GIVING VOICE TO STONES

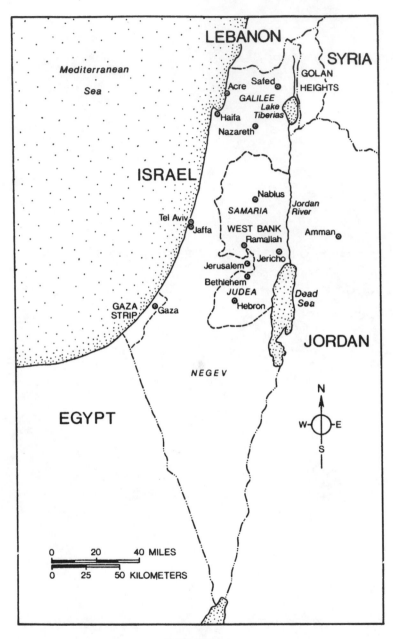

Israel/Palestine

GIVING VOICE
TO STONES

Place and Identity in Palestinian Literature

~

BARBARA McKEAN PARMENTER

UNIVERSITY OF TEXAS PRESS
AUSTIN

First edition, 1994

Requests for permission to reproduce material from this work
should be sent to Permissions, University of Texas Press, Box 7819,
Austin, TX, 78713-7819.

◎ The paper used in this publication meets the minimum
requirements of American National Standard for Information
Sciences—Permanence of Paper for Printed Library Materials, ANSI
Z39.48-1984

LIBRARY OF CONGRESS CATALOGING-IN-PUBLICATION DATA

Parmenter, Barbara M., date
    Giving voice to stones : place and identity in Palestinian
literature / Barbara McKean Parmenter. — 1st ed.
        p.   cm
    Includes bibliographical references and index.
    ISBN 0-292-72751-8 (alk. paper). — ISBN 0-292-76555-X (pbk. :
alk. paper)
    1. Arabic literature—Palestine—History and criticism.
2. Geographical perception in literature. 3. Arabic
literature—1801– —History and criticism. 4. Palestine in
literature. 5. Palestinian Arabs—Ethnic identity. I. Title.
PJ8190.P3P37 1994
892'.70995694—dc20   94-8643

CONTENTS

PREFACE AND ACKNOWLEDGMENTS
VII

ONE
THE MEANING OF STONES
I

TWO
READING THE LANDSCAPE
*Images of Palestine in the Nineteenth
and Early Twentieth Centuries*
8

THREE
THE LITERATURE OF STRUGGLE AND LOSS
1920–1960
28

FOUR
LANDSCAPES OF EXILE
48

FIVE

LANDSCAPES OF HOME

70

SIX

ENCOUNTERING ISRAEL

86

NOTES

99

BIBLIOGRAPHY

109

INDEX

115

PREFACE AND
ACKNOWLEDGMENTS

This book is a very personal interpretation of Palestinian literature and its evocation of land, home, and place. From my first encounter with the poetry and prose of Palestine I have been struck by the struggle of Palestinian authors to define the meanings and experiences of place and identity. After having read countless books about the Arab-Israeli conflict, reading the words of Palestinians themselves illuminated issues in a new and immeasurably more encompassing light. I do not pretend to present a complete survey of Palestinian literature, nor of the Palestinian experience. Rather, this is one reading of the literature which I hope will provide some insights and understanding. I fully realize that others will have very different interpretations, which is as it should be. I would like to add that this book is deliberately one-sided in the sense that it focuses on Palestinian literature and deals only in passing with Hebrew literature. I felt that Israeli experiences of land and home are well represented in English-language books, and that I could not substantially add to those analyses. I have used several of these works on Hebrew literature and include them in the references for readers who are interested.

Many translated selections of Arabic poetry and prose appear in this book. In some instances, I have used previously published English translations. For these selections, the reference note gives the English title of the work and the name of the author as it appears in the published edition. All other Arabic translations are my own and I am solely responsible for any errors. For these selections, I have transliterated the Arabic title and the author's name as they would appear in a library catalog, but without the standard diacritical marks. All Hebrew selections are from published English translations. In general, Arabic and Hebrew words have been transliterated in a way which I hope will make them both readable and reasonably accurate.

This book has benefited from the advice and involvement of many individuals. First and foremost, I am especially indebted to Robin W. Doughty and Ian R. Manners of the Department of Geography at The University of Texas at Austin for their encouragement and painstaking critiques of the manuscript. Their patience and perseverance saw me through the process of turning a few disparate ideas concerning geography, place, and Arabic literature into a finished book. Numerous other colleagues at The University of Texas and elsewhere also gave their time, suggestions, and encouragement, including Elizabeth Fernea, Doug Barnett, Zjaleh Hajibashi, Ann Helgeson, Ted Swedenburg, and Susan Slyomovics. Makram Copty recommended Palestinian authors and critics and was always ready to help with suggestions, difficult passages, and general reassurances that I wasn't too far off track. John Cotter produced a map in record time and saved me from putting my cartographic skills to the test. Jeff Larsen, Tamsen Donner, John Rando, Kathryn Burns, and Victoria Wing sustained me with unending good humor and companionship while I was writing the original manuscript. Ann Walther was a prime catalyst for this book through her relentless insistence that I not file the manuscript away in a drawer. She is a dear friend for whose judgment and support I am extremely grateful.

I would like to thank the staff at the University of Texas Press for their work and commitment to this manuscript, and I especially thank Helen Hyams for her careful editing. I am also indebted to the readers who anonymously reviewed the draft for their constructive criticisms and corrections. Despite this wealth of aid and support, I of course take sole responsibility for any errors of fact, omission, or interpretation.

There are four people whose teaching and support have been

critical to my growth and particularly to my understanding of language and literature. First, I would like to express my deep appreciation to Farouk Mustafa of the University of Chicago with whom I spent many, many hours studying Arabic literature over the course of three years as an undergraduate. He is a champion teacher and mentor who opened up a new language and world to me. I would also like to thank Mrs. Narriman Warraki, of the American University in Cairo, who first introduced me to the literature of Palestine, her native land, in a way that was honest, insightful, and free of dogma. Finally, I offer my deepest gratitude to my mother and father, who sent me on a tour of the Holy Land as a teenager and who encouraged me to study non-European languages and literature, even at that young age, to expand my horizons of knowledge. They were multiculturalists long before the term was coined.

CHAPTER I

THE MEANING OF STONES

Palestinian poet Mahmud Darwish reflected on the meaning of home in a book of essays published in the early 1970s, shortly after he left Israel for a life in exile. In one passage, he addressed the following words to Israelis:

> The true homeland is not that which is known or proved. The land which emerges as if from a chemical equation or an institute of theory is not a homeland. Your insistent need to demonstrate the history of stones and your ability to invent proofs does not give you prior membership over him who knows the time of the rain from the smell of the stone. That stone for you is an intellectual effort. For its owner it is a roof and walls.[1]

For Darwish, the encounter between Palestinian and Israeli perceptions of homeland cuts to the core of what he calls "a struggle between two memories." The significance of stones weaves through this struggle. For Zionists, the history of the Land of Israel was written in its stones, and archaeology became not just a national passion but a means to construct a link between contemporary Jews and an ancient tribal territory, in order to rebuild Jewish identity as Israeli identity. For Darwish, stones encompass the very substance of Palestinian life, the roof and walls which form an unspoken, existential bond between people and place. The Israelis reduced the roof and walls of Darwish's childhood home to rubble and refused to let its inhabitants return to their former lands. Visiting the site as an adult, Darwish encounters a young Jewish shepherd, an immigrant from Yemen, who hails him. "Are you from Yemen?" the boy asks. When Darwish tells him that he was born where they are standing, the boy is astounded. "He thought the mounds of rubble were the ruins of a Roman village," Darwish says.[2]

Beginning in December 1987, the "children of the stones," the younger generation of Palestinians raised under occupation, brought the struggle to a new level in the Intifada, the uprising. The very stones so steeped in history for Israelis were carefully gathered and cached as weapons of resistance. The Intifada turned the encounter between David and Goliath, part of Israel's national mythology of a small community pitted against giants, on its head. At the same time it shattered the symbol-laden rhetoric of the older generation of Palestinians which had evolved through decades of encounter with Israelis.

The struggle over stones is part of a wider rhetorical battle about the meaning of land, home, and place. This book examines the evolution of a Palestinian "land rhetoric" as expressed in Palestinian literature since the First World War until the advent of the Intifada. I take the term *land rhetoric* from Raja Shehadeh's very enlightening discussion of how Israel has changed the way he perceives his surroundings, in his book, *The Third Way*.[3]

As a geographer, I began this study out of an intense interest in the meaning and experience of place. What defines a place as opposed to undefined space? What sets places apart from each other and why are they so important for people? Clearly these questions involve a complex spectrum of factors ranging from aspects of the biophysical environment to social and power relationships between individuals and communities. Just as clearly, these questions are not unique to the experiences of Israelis and Palestinians.

In our popular culture, we express a remarkable desire to see the Middle East as a region of irrational and chronic tribal feuding, a land where conflict uniquely inheres in the nature of people and environment. In this view, the struggle between Arabs and Israelis plays out ancient rivalries between natural enemies. There is, however, little unique about conflict in the Middle East, or about power struggles over territory and identity. As I write these words, I survey a landscape of fences and yards occupying land once inhabited by people I know little about—Tonkawas, Comanches, and others whose voices were silenced over a century ago. Every day brings news of social and ethnic upheavals in Europe, Asia, Africa, and the streets of America. Although technology has surpassed all the necessary requirements for the development of a "global village," what we see and experience at the end of the twentieth century is a resurgence of local, place-bound tribalism as we and others jockey for position in an era of shifting power relationships.

What is perhaps unique about the encounter between Israelis and Palestinians is the degree of articulation about the significance of place. Both sides have long engaged in intensive propaganda campaigns to delineate and justify claims to territory. But beyond the propaganda lies a rich vein of thought exploring the links between people and place. Beginning without territory, the Zionist vision of place could only express itself in the realm of words as a means of empowerment and persuasion. As the success of Zionism dispossessed Palestinians of land and of hope for independence, so the Palestinians' vision of place came also to be expressed in writing, recorded for their own people and presented to the world. The struggle between these two ways of speaking has in turn transformed their meanings. Palestinians and Jews both bear the distinguishing mark of refugees, Darwish observes, and "now, each contributes to giving form to the other. . . . What brings us together is at the same time a point of conflict between us."[4] In exploring this tension we find insights about both the human experience of place and the political uses to which this experience is put.

THE GEOGRAPHY OF PLACE

Because this study grew out of an interest in the study of place, a brief introduction to this field of inquiry is in order. *Place* is defined as a segment of space which an individual or group imbues with special meaning, value, and intention.[5] As such, it is a key concept in humanistic studies in geography, planning, and architecture. Many writers have explored the experience of place in industrialized Western societies, focusing especially on the individual's growing alienation from his or her "place" in the world. Architect Christopher Alexander and colleagues have attempted to define the essential qualities of places which make meaningful and positive experience possible.[6] Others have also explored what they believe to be the essential experiences of place, often couching their discussions in terms of paired oppositions. Anne Buttimer suggests that "we think of place in the context of two reciprocal movements: [the need for] home and horizons of reach outward from that home."[7] Kevin Lynch, whose 1960 book, *The Image of the City,* became a focal point for debate among urban designers, argues that satisfying places must be both legible and diverse.[8] Jay Appleton takes the perspective of animal behavior and speaks of the concomitant need for both refuge (home) and prospect (the ability to survey and take advantage of one's surroundings).[9] And Edward Relph writes that to experience place as home provides "a point of departure from which we orient ourselves and take possession of the world."[10] These paired oppositions are frequently seen as essential in human nature expressed in the human body. Relph and others, for example, argue that the essence of place lies in the "experience of an 'inside' that is distinct from an 'outside.' "[11]

Yi-Fu Tuan, a geographer who has investigated cross-cultural notions of place, admits of universally held oppositions like left and right or up and down, but goes on to distinguish between two ways of experiencing place—"rootedness" and "sense of place." Rootedness is unself-conscious and implies "an incuriosity toward the world at large and an insensitivity toward the flow of time." It is being at home without having to think about it. To have a sense of place, on the other hand, is to self-consciously construct an attachment to and appreciation of the local environment. The latter requires a certain distance between self and place, together with an acute awareness of the outside world and the flow of time. Tuan remarks on the use of historical events to construct a sense of place but stops short of analyzing the dynamics of this process. The implication is that place, or at least a sense of place, is a social construct as well as an existential experience.[12]

This distinction appears frequently in discussions of Martin Heidegger's writing on how humans dwell in the world. For Heidegger, the vernacular farmhouse architecture of the Black Forest manifests an authentic way of dwelling because its form embodies the lived experience of its inhabitants.[13]

Social critics of Heidegger's ideas note how the Nazis employed similar visions of authentic human living for purely political and ultimately horrific ends. For critics, there can be no universal, essential ways of experiencing place. Any attempt to claim that there are serves to obfuscate social realities and buttress an ideological agenda by portraying it as natural. Australian architect Kim Dovey argues that a dialogue between essentialists and relativists about our understanding of place could offer insights too often overlooked by proponents of one approach or the other.[14]

A study of literature aids in understanding both the terms of this discussion and the substantive meanings of place. Literature articulates the human experiences of daily life that are normally left implicit and unarticulated. Like science, literature is a means of ordering the world, but it does so in a way that retains what philosopher Maurice Natanson calls "thick experience, the world of our errors and confusions as well as of our victories and insights." This contrasts with the "clean reality" found in the scientific ordering of the world.[15]

Perceptive Palestinian and Israeli observers articulate the thick experience of place. While others try to deny a confusing reality that does not fit with authoritative viewpoints, these writers recognize the existence of two interweaving and opposing places within the area controlled by Israel. Israeli journalist Uri Avneri remarks that in his conversations with Palestinians, a map of the land emerges which is entirely different from his own:

> In every meeting a map is drawn—not the map of today, but the map from the Mandate period—when Shlomi was Basa, and Kiryat Shemona was Khalsa, and Ashdod was Asdud. . . . After three generations, nothing has been erased; on the contrary, it has been

sharpened. . . . It will never be easy to solve the problem of a man who dreams about his house and the trees of [his village], even if he has never seen them.[16]

Palestinian poet Layla 'Allush, in "The Path of Affection," reflects on the features of her Palestine which still survive within the newly imposed landscape of Israel:

Along the amazing road drawn from the throat of recent
  dates . . .
Along the amazing road drawn from my old Jerusalem,
And despite the hybrid signs, shops, and cemeteries,
My fragmented self drew together to meet the kin of New
  Haifa. . . .
The earth remained unchanged as of old,
With all its mortgaged trees dotting the hills,
And all the green clouds and the plants
Fertilized with fresh fertilizers,
And efficient sprinklers. . . .
In the earth there was an apology for my father's wounds,
And all along the bridges was my Arab countenance,
In the tall poplars,
In the trains and windows,
In the smoke rings.
Everything is Arab despite the change of tongue,
Despite the trucks, the cars, and the car lights. . . .
All the poplars and my ancestor's solemn orchards
Were, I swear, smiling at me with Arab affection.
Despite all that had been eliminated and coordinated and the
  "modern" sounds . . .
Despite the seas of light and technology. . . .
O my grandparents, the rich soil was bright with Arab reserve,
And it sang out, believe me, with affection.[17]

'Allush finds in the current landscape remnant features whose meanings remain sufficiently strong to sing out over the noise of the new, technologically coordinated landscape of Israel. These are the meanings which enable the Palestinians about whom Avneri writes to still speak of their homes as acutely present, even in their absence. In these words we begin to discern the geography of an existential Palestine.

CHAPTER 2

READING THE LANDSCAPE

*Images of Palestine in the Nineteenth
and Early Twentieth Centuries*

Visions of a past Palestine continue to shape the contemporary land rhetoric, not only for Palestinians and Israelis, but for external political powers to whom both sides look for support. The bases for the current struggle between memories developed during the nineteenth and early twentieth centuries, first with the "rediscovery" of Palestine by Western travelers, archaeologists, and biblical historians, and then with the founding of the Zionist movement. It is to this period also that Palestinians look back in efforts to anchor their own land rhetoric. To understand the present we must explore at least the general outlines of this past landscape, and the meanings with which it was imbued.

WESTERN IMAGES OF PALESTINE

Europeans and Americans took a keen interest in Palestine during the nineteenth century. Between 1800 and 1878 they published an estimated 5,000 books and articles dealing with the area.[1] The Near East in general was of growing strategic importance as European governments vied for position in anticipation of the Ottoman Empire's demise. Palestine attracted particular attention by merit of its biblical history. It was the "Holy Land," the cradle of the Judeo-Christian world. The renewed popular interest in

Palestine resulted from several factors. Increasing European in-
tervention in the Ottoman Empire made the region more acces-
sible to Western visitors. Adventurers, missionaries, explorers, and
tourists were eager to visit a country possessing such powerful
associations with their religious and cultural heritage. On a more
dogmatic level, the Enlightenment's insistence on scientific ex-
planation had raised questions concerning the validity of biblical
writings. Defenders of both faith and science felt that they could
demonstrate the truths of the Bible through archaeological and
ethnographic explorations in the Holy Land. In addition, the apparent disparity between ancient descriptions of the land's prosperity and its poor condition under Ottoman rule created a desire
to "regenerate" Palestine, an idea which reflected the eighteenth
and nineteenth century's obsession with innovation and improvement in agriculture and industry. This ideal reinforced religious
aspirations to Christianize (or later Judaize) Palestine in fulfillment of biblical prophecies.

All these factors played a role in shaping the Western image of
Palestine well before the establishment of the British Mandate in
1920. When Americans and Europeans traveled to the Holy Land,
they carried in their minds a preformed landscape based on their
own cultural upbringing and experiences. Many were disap-
pointed when they compared their expectations with the contemporary reality they encountered. Ruins lay everywhere, towns
looked strange and dangerous, villages were impoverished, and
agriculture appeared hopelessly backward. The inhabitants, who
for the most part did not share the Christian faith, seemed unworthy inheritors of so sacred a legacy. A letter to the *Times* of
London, reprinted in the *Palestine Exploration Fund Quarterly
Statement* in 1880, exemplifies this type of reaction:

> Nothing can well exceed the desolateness of much of it. Treeless it
> is for 20 or 30 miles together, forests which did exist 30 years ago
> fast disappearing, rich plains of the finest garden soil asking to be
> cultivated, at best but scratched up a few inches deep in patches,
> with no hedges or boundaries, mountain terraces ready to be
> planted with vines, as the German colony are doing at the foot of
> Mount Carmel; the villages nothing but mud huts, dust, dirt, and

squalor; the inhabitants with scarce clothing enough for decency, their houses—ovens; large tracts without a horse or cow, sheep or dog; no pretence at roads except from Jaffa to Jerusalem, and this like a cart road over a ploughed field, the rest at best like sheepwalks on the Downs of Sussex, but for the most part like the dry bed of the most rocky river, where amid blocks of stone each makes his way at a footpace as best he can . . . or over loose stones thrown down from the old walls on either side, which no one offers a finger to remove; nothing upon wheels, not so much as a barrow, to be met with in a ride of over three hundred miles. . . . Nothing like a small farmhouse is to be found far or near. . . . The towns are filthy in the extreme, none more so than Jerusalem itself. . . . This is a picture, I believe, in no way overdrawn, of that land which was once "flowing with milk and honey."[2]

It is clearly the English landscape which has given shape to the author's idea of what the Holy Land should look like. He draws images from the Bible, inserts them into a context drawn from English ideals of a pastoral society (gardens, hedges, small farms), and proceeds to condemn the reality he finds for not living up to his expectations. The inhabitants are paupers in rags who live in "ovens" and whose works are worthless. What they do, what they experience, and what meanings they give the land on which they live are ignored and thereby removed from the picture. The implication is that the present population is undeserving of the land. The author confirms this judgment in his conclusion:

Blessed indeed will that power surely be which shall first move to establish some such international company for the purchase and government of Palestine—not seeking in any way its own aggrandizement, but perhaps, thus fulfilling in a way beyond what is ordinary or common, our daily prayer, "Thy will be done on Earth as it is in Heaven" for "Jerusalem shall be trodden down of the Gentiles until the times of the Gentiles be fulfilled."[3]

Thus do capital improvement and biblical prophecy combine to rob a land and people of their own identity. Others who visited or lived in Palestine responded to it in similar ways. W. M. Thomson, a missionary in Palestine in the mid–nineteenth century and author of *The Land and the Book*, quotes Josephus's glowing description of the Galilee region and then comments:

> The soil may be as good as ever, the climate the same, but where are the walnuts, the figs, the olives, the grapes and the other fruits? . . . Alas! all gone . . . and there are no inhabitants . . . to cultivate this "ambition of Nature."[4]

Clinging to a priori images of the land, many travelers viewed the contemporary landscape as the flotsam of centuries of neglect burying the "true" Palestine. To see the Holy Land, one had to look beneath the rubble; to reclaim it one had to remove the debris. Professional and amateur archaeologists ranged through these ruins. Tourists flocked from one holy site to another. Explorers surveyed the region, mapped the scenes of its ancient history, and meticulously recorded the land's topography, geology, flora, and fauna, comparing and contrasting them all the while with ancient writings. The results encouraged Christian and Jewish groups interested in establishing missions and agricultural colonies in Palestine. The land's spiritual and physical potential was ripe and its native residents apparently unable or unwilling to reap the harvest.

This "archaeological" vision of the land and its people supported later Zionist claims by providing links between the Bible and the contemporary landscape. Meron Benvenisti notes that American Edward Robinson's efforts in the nineteenth century to match contemporary Arab place names with biblical equivalents created the basis for the map of Israel in the twentieth. The Arabs had clung to these indigenous, Semitic names through long periods of foreign rule. By doing so, they made possible biblical reconstruction and subsequent Israeli possession. The irony is not lost on Benvenisti. "Paradoxically enough," he notes, "the skeleton of the Hebrew map of Israel was immortalized and preserved by that same people whose own place names we sought to erase."[5]

The irony is lost on others. Israeli geographer Yehoshua Ben-Arieh, in his book, *The Rediscovery of the Holy Land in the Nineteenth Century*, lauds the explorers, travelers, and archaeologists who dedicated themselves to "uncover[ing] the secrets of the Holy Land," not from imperialist desires but for purposes of scientific research.[6] The idea that the true Palestine lay buried beneath the rubble of the contemporary scene is now so widespread that the assumption of a Holy Land with secrets waiting to be uncovered by Western science often goes unquestioned. Ben-Arieh argues that in Palestine,

> the unknown was somehow familiar. The Bible, Josephus, the writings of the church fathers, crusader chronicles—all seemed to come alive out of the *dusty ruins* and the *forsaken landscape*. To this day, archaeological discoveries in Israel have this forsaken quality about them. The same spirit permeated even the study of the physical characteristics and the natural history of Palestine.[7] (emphasis added)

Not all Westerners dismissed the contemporary land and life of Palestine as rubble to be excavated. In contrast to the archaeological approach is the ethnographic encounter. This view of the Holy Land presents the landscape and its inhabitants as picturesque examples of biblical stories and events. This was Thomson's aim in his book describing Palestine circa 1857, which he subtitled, "Biblical Illustrations Drawn from the Manners and Customs, the Scenes and Scenery of the Holy Land." It included an index of illustrated scriptural texts.[8] The book went through several editions and became a favorite among American Sunday-school teachers.

G. Robinson Lees takes this ethnographic approach in his book, *Village Life in Palestine*. In its preface he argues for the importance of looking at contemporary people and place:

> At a time when the Bible is the object of severe textual criticism I hope it will not be thought inopportune to urge for consideration the confirmatory evidence of the truth of the Bible supplied by the life of the people in the land of the Bible.[9]

The ethnographic approach disputes the archaeological image of "dusty ruins" and "the forsaken landscape." In these tomes the land is far from empty. Lees, for example, chastises those who write only of the desolation of Palestine, suggesting that these travelers have not thoroughly explored the territory. The poor condition of the country has been overestimated, he claims, and the current landscape has much to tell of the past. The Arab inhabitants are "the descendents of the mixed marriages of the children of Israel with the aboriginal inhabitants of the country, through whom they were led into sin and idolatry." They are, he continues, the inhabitants described in the Second Book of Kings as "the poorest sort of people," who were left to be "vinedressers and husbandmen" when the Hebrews were carried into captivity.[10] Lees's book also contains photographs illustrating the Bible with captions such as "The Good Shepherd," "The Sower," and "The Watchman." Attaching biblical labels to photographs of daily life in Palestine was a popular technique for illustrating religious books and postcards. To make sure that the reader made the correct connection, scriptural references were frequently added.[11]

This type of literature often portrays Palestinian society sympathetically, yet it still presents a Western picture. Instead of ignoring or condemning the contemporary culture, these writers and travelers incorporate it into their preformed images by abstracting the inhabitants from their own personal lives and experiences and inserting them into biblical contexts. Palestine is thus isolated from history and becomes a timeless, changeless place confirming the word of God as interpreted by the Western observer. Thomson views Palestine as "one vast table whereupon God's messages to men have been drawn, and graven deep in living characters by the Great Publisher of glad tidings, to be seen and read to the end of time."[12] Palestinian society, therefore, exists to teach us about *our* Holy Land. Rather than portraying the land and people as products of their own history, they become figures in ours.

Even sympathetic descriptions of Palestine often depicted the lives of its inhabitants in terms that appeared irrationally conservative when viewed from a Western capitalist perspective. Sarah Graham-Brown notes this in regard to early photography of Palestinian life. "A simple plough or threshing board 'as used in biblical times,' " she argues, "symbolized backwardness, quaint and picturesque as it might be." It was seldom mentioned, she continues, that the plough in question might be well suited to the environment or that few peasants could afford equipment not made locally. Instead, ignorance, stupidity, and conservatism were put forward as explanations.[13] This view continues to influence current attempts to reconstruct the land and life of Palestine prior to the British Mandate. Jacob Landau, author of several books about the Arabs, claims:

> The most easily discernible characteristic of nineteenth century Palestine was change-resistant conservatism. . . . In terms of material culture, this attitude was expressed in resistance to the renewal of equipment or apparel, which was never willingly discarded until hopelessly worn—and the new purchase was a repeat of the discarded article. Once again, this was merely symptomatic of an almost general antipathy, or apathy to innovation.[14]

Here, what in its own context is eminently rational, and even admirable, behavior becomes antipathetic or just plain lazy when put into the framework of European market economies.

Both the archaeological and ethnographic approaches posit a direct relationship between the landscape and its Western chroniclers (and their readers) which ignores or reduces the experiences of those who actually dwell in the land. James Turner, in an analysis of English topographic poetry, speaks of "symbolic possession," in which the "imaginary possession-by-description of an actual landscape becomes a morally superior substitute for the real estate it both emulates and reviles."[15] By figuratively removing contemporary residents from the Western image of the Holy Land or incorporating them into it, the legions of surveyors, historians, and naturalists who combed Palestine in the nineteenth century symbolically possessed the land long before the British took political control of it. This situation was in no way unique. Much the same was happening in colonized lands around the globe. In Palestine, the long-term implications were profound. Economic and political aims resonated with emotional and spiritual meaning for both Christians and Jews. While geographies, maps, and specimen collections from other lands gathered dust on the shelves of colonial libraries, the Zionist movement breathed new life into the works of nineteenth-century Westerners in Palestine. Their interpretations of the land provided a foothold for a new form of possession.

PALESTINE AND ZIONISM

The Zionist image of Palestine, while partaking of more general European perspectives, contained unique aspects arising from the religious traditions and the historical experience of European Jewry. Eretz Israel, the land of Israel, and Zion, the ideal community of the Jews, are central concepts in Judaism. The status of the Jews as the chosen people of God arises from their covenant with God in which they were given Eretz Israel. The ingathering of exiles in Zion, to be accomplished by the Messiah, represents the final redemption of the Jews. Thus, as with Western Gentiles, the Jewish vision of the Holy Land was an amalgam of a biblical past and an anticipated future. Unlike the Gentiles, however, the Jews considered themselves to be in exile; thus, the return to Zion promised personal and communal redemption in fulfillment of prophecy. Discrimination against Jews and their persecution in Europe served only to reinforce the experience of exile and increase the yearning for Zion.[16]

The return to Zion, however, was not necessarily physical. Many religious Jews envisioned Zion as a spiritual ingathering rather than a bodily return to Eretz Israel. Hillel Bavli notes that

> Zion, as envisioned by the poets of the nineteenth century, was mainly a legendary character, a sublime illusion, a religious ecstasy. In the words of the poet Micah Joseph Lebenson it was: "The land where the muses dwell, where each flower is a Psalm, each cedar a song divine, each stone a book and each rock a tablet."[17]

This mystical vision is similar to that of Thomson in reflecting biblical images rather than geographic reality. As hopes for Jewish political and cultural emancipation faded in the face of increasing persecution, particularly in Russia, during the latter half of the nineteenth century, new visions of Zion emerged. Anti-Semitism, the rise of nationalism, and the Romantic ideal of nature and agrarian life gave birth to Zionism, which advocated the establishment of a homeland for Jews on their own territory.

An early wave of emigration to Palestine began in Russia in 1882. The Hibbat Zion (Love of Zion) movement, founded in Russia in 1884, encouraged this emigration as a means of "auto-emancipation" for Russian Jews. These middle-class, mostly middle-aged immigrants established agricultural colonies called *moshavot*, funded in large part by philanthropist and banker Baron Edmund de Rothschild. Rothschild's autocratic style and insistence on direct administrative control frustrated many of the colonists, who nevertheless depended on his largesse. Most of these settlements were in the coastal plain or in Galilee in northern Palestine. By the turn of the century, many had become colonial-style plantations employing large numbers of Arab workers, a situation that dismayed some Zionists, including members of Hibbat Zion.[18]

By 1897, the year of the First Zionist Congress in Vienna, Theodor Herzl and others had articulated a more political and ideological program for a new Jewish homeland. Herzl argued that Jews were an abnormal nation because they possessed no territorial base. By establishing a Jewish state within a circumscribed geographic area, the Jews could transform themselves into a true nation with all the attendant properties which national status conveys. Continuing persecution in Russia and Eastern Europe exemplified the Jews' lack of national standing and made the selection of a site more urgent. Herzl was prepared to negotiate on this latter point, and briefly considered Northern Sinai, Cyprus, and Uganda, all British colonial possessions.[19]

The Uganda plan came closest to fruition and caused a deep crisis for Zionists, who preferred Palestine because of its obvious historical and emotional significance. Some also argued that Palestine was an apparent territorial vacuum in the declining Ottoman Empire, a backwater to which no other people were attracted.[20] The early slogan, "A land without people for a people without land," reflected the popular image in the West of a ruined and forsaken Holy Land. Most Zionists recognized the literal falsity of the empty-land argument and acknowledged the presence of Arab inhabitants. Yet even if Palestine was not empty, it still appeared to be a vacuum in the sense that it was not a nation. Its people were attached to their villages and clans, but Zionists believed the inhabitants lacked a sense of larger unity. Although some Zionists argued for coexistence between Arabs and Jews, others believed that the current residents could be persuaded to move, especially with the inflated offers Jewish buyers were offering for land.[21]

Toward the end of the nineteenth century, revolutionary upheaval in Europe and agrarian ideals of an intimate bond between nature and folk began to exert a profound influence on the Zionist vision of Palestine. This influence was especially strong during the second distinct wave of Jewish immigration into Palestine between 1904 and 1914, known as the Second Aliyah (Ascent). Steeped in both socialist and Romantic thought, these new immigrants concurred with Herzl on the need to root a new Jewish nation in territory, but not only for the political status gained thereby. Zionist socialists viewed the alienating and suffocating life of urban ghettos with disgust.[22] Micah Joseph Berdichevsky, an important figure in Hebrew literature during the late nineteenth and early twentieth centuries, wrote that the ghetto Jews of Europe were "not a nation, not a people, not human." Yosef Haim Brenner, a radical critic of European Jewry, called the ghetto Jews "gypsies and filthy dogs."[23] For the new immigrants, working the land was not simply a way to establish the territorial foundation of nationhood but a path of active secular redemption from this abject degradation. Berdichevsky spoke poignantly of the deep need for attachment to soil:

> We lack a foundation in whatever we build, our heavenly sanctities lack a firm horizon; our souls, our very breath lacks soil; our poetry, our ideas lack inhabited ground . . . no abstract culture can endure for any length of time if it is not nourished and sustained by earth.[24]

Unlike European Christians, who viewed the Holy Land as needing regeneration, Zionists saw the land as the means for regenerating the Jewish people. Through caring and loving labor on the soil of their ancient territory, Jews could renew their bond with the earth and rid their culture of its encrusted urban ghetto mentality. The new Jews could then stand strong among the peoples of the world and be a shining light of social justice.

This investment of the land with profound redemptive powers raised inevitable tensions when it was put into practice. Socialist Zionists challenged what they saw as the bourgeois practices of older Jewish landowners who routinely employed Arab workers. Many argued that social redemption required pure Jewish labor on Jewish land, lest the Jews in Palestine become incorporated into the exploitative landowning classes. For the landowners, the utopian vision of the newcomers was unreasonable and impractical. Arab workers were acclimated to environmental conditions, performed their jobs better, and demanded less than the young ideologues fresh from Europe. The labor issue became the subject of a continuing and heated controversy among Zionists, for both its economic and cultural significance.[25]

The vision of Jewish revival through labor on the land led to the formation of the Jewish National Fund in 1901 to purchase, develop, and settle land in Palestine. Once it was purchased by the Fund, the land became the inalienable property of the Jewish people. No settler could dispose of his lease to a non-Jew, and any tenants who employed Arab labor were fined and threatened with eviction.[26]

These policies were bound to cause tensions with the Arabs in Palestine, yet only a few foresaw the potential for intractable conflict between the two communities. As early as 1891, Ahad Ha'am had shocked Zionist circles in Europe and new immigrants in Palestine with his warning that the Arabs of Palestine would resist the usurpation of their rights.[27] In 1905, Itzhak Epstein sparked angry responses when he argued at the Seventh Zionist Congress that Palestine was not empty, that its Arab inhabitants were indeed a nation, and that Zionism confronted a vexing moral issue in displacing these native inhabitants.[28]

Some responded to Epstein by remonstrating that Jewish concerns for the rights of other peoples had rarely been returned in kind, and that it was time to stand up for Jewish rights just as other European nationalities were doing. Others argued that the Arabs of Palestine were not a nation but a band of warring tribes who threatened the existence of Jewish settlements. Still others, including Herzl, remonstrated that the native Arabs of Palestine would soon realize the blessings of Jewish immigration and enterprise. The new Jewish homeland would lift the country and its people out of the ruins created by centuries of Ottoman neglect and exploitation. There would be new opportunities for work and industry, as well as all the other attendant benefits of modernization. The Arabs, realizing this, would then gladly acquiesce to Jewish leadership. For many who shared these views, it was the upper-class Arabs who were stirring up opposition to Zionism, fearing competition and displacement from the traditional power structure which allowed them to exploit the peasantry. The mass of the population, on the other hand, could only benefit from Jewish land ownership.[29]

This misapprehension of the impact of Zionist activities in Palestine on its Arab inhabitants can be attributed to many factors, and Zionists argued among themselves concerning the correct position to take toward the Arabs. Their perspectives on local Arab communities were varied, ambiguous, and often conflicting. Literary critic Gila Ramras-Rauch, in her study of Arabs in Israeli literature, argues that early Zionists feared, abhorred, and envied the Palestinian Arabs. The latter appeared both loathsome and pitiful in their poverty and backwardness, and sometimes outright hostile. Yet for several Zionist writers, Arabs also represented what Jewish immigrants so desperately wanted—they were the native sons of the soil, and they appeared to have an intimate bond with the land.

In much of pre-1948 Jewish literature, the Arab is part and parcel of the landscape, a symbol of rootedness for rootless immigrants yearning to establish their own home. Some writers saw the nomadic Bedouins as a living example of the biblical tribes of Israel. For young Zionists wanting to cleanse their culture of its ghetto mentality, the Bedouins were alluringly exotic, wild, and in touch with the harsh desert in a primal way. In other instances, the romanticization of Bedouin nomads and Arab peasants carried with it a clear and condescending paternalism. The Arab, although rooted, lacked the energy and skills to make something of the land, and therefore it was up to the Jews to redeem the soil. In doing so they would lift up the poor Arabs' lives as well. Others, notably Yosef Haim Brenner, perceived the inherent conflict. For Brenner, the Arab became lodged in the Jewish psyche both as an example of the bond between people and place and as a looming threat to the realization of a Jewish homeland. At least one Zionist, Nissim Malul, a Palestine-born Sephardic Jew, called for total Jewish integration with Arab culture as the only basis for creating a true Hebrew culture free of European influence. This prefigures in certain respects the later emergence of the Canaanite movement in Israel, which seeks a prebiblical basis for a Hebrew nation. The ambivalent position of the Arab as enemy and native son remains to this day a vexing issue in both Israeli literature and politics.[30]

The Zionist vision of Palestine as Jewish homeland thus shared in the popular imagery of the West and differed from it in certain fundamental respects. Nonetheless, it also represented a symbolic possession of the land. Hillel Bavli refers to the literary "reclamation" of Zion:

> The physical characteristics of the land, its variegated landscape, its flora and fauna and its deserts have become potent factors coloring greatly the poetry of Israel. In truth one may say that the land of Israel in its fullness was reclaimed poetically long before it was reclaimed politically.[31]

Note that this poetic landscape lacks any reference to the existing society of Palestine. While a few writers grappled with the vexing question of the Arabs, the main thrust of Zionist writings, like those of Western Christians, made the native people invisible. They were considered unworthy of the land or irrationally hostile, or they were incorporated into the native scenery along with the other fauna.

In 1920 and 1921, Arabs rioted in Jerusalem and Jaffa. Ninety-five people died in the Jaffa disturbances before British troops restored order. According to historian Walter Laquer, these riots "shocked and confused the Zionists [as] many of them became aware for the first time of the danger of a major conflict" between Arab and Jew. Laquer labeled this the "unseen question"—the sudden appearance of a formerly invisible but angry people.[32] Although few had ever believed the notion of a literally empty Palestine, its symbolic reclamation had allowed it to be portrayed as figuratively empty. In this figurative sense, the belief that Palestine was "a land without people" persists. In 1969, for example, Prime Minister Golda Meir argued that when the Zionists arrived in Palestine,

> there was no such thing as Palestinians. . . . It was not as though there was a Palestinian people in Palestine considering itself as a Palestinian people and we came and threw them out and took their country away from them. They did not exist.[33]

In one sense she was right. There was no Palestine in the Western sense of a nation-state and no Palestinian people in the Western sense of a national group taking explicit possession of and improving its national territory. By Western definition, Palestinians, like many other native peoples around the world, did not exist.

PALESTINE AND
THE PALESTINIAN ARABS

Who were these people, then, who inhabited the land, who were alternately brushed aside as rubble or romanticized as biblical native sons? What significance did the land hold for them and what meanings did they give to different aspects of their environment? Although the reconstruction of the pre-Zionist landscape of Palestine is an ultimately impossible task, we must explore its general outline if we are to understand how contemporary Palestinians view their land. Due to the country's isolation from the cultural mainstreams of the Arab world, however, Palestine produced few indigenous writers until the twentieth century.[34] Thus native literature is scarce and foreign writings must be drawn on to some extent. Folklore offers another means for examining the subjective experience of place among a largely nonliterate people. Contemporary Palestinian scholars and activists have, in fact, attached great significance to collecting various aspects of folklore as a means of reconstructing and preserving pre-Zionist Palestinian culture. Although the usefulness of folklore is limited because it covers only certain aspects of society and culture, it can nonetheless offer important insights.

Nineteenth-century Palestinians strongly identified with their local town or village. Jerusalem, Gaza, Nablus, Jaffa, Acre, Hebron, and Safed were the largest towns. Each had one or two important families with whom the town's identity was invariably linked. Clothing, particularly the embroidery patterns on women's dresses, also linked people with a town and its local region. In addition, most towns were well known for their distinctive occupational specialties. The artisans of Gaza excelled in weaving and pottery, Nablus was the most important soap-making and textile center, the people of Hebron specialized in viticulture and in the manufacture of glassware and waterbags, Nazareth produced agricultural implements, and Bethlehem was famous for its fine stonemasons and skilled builders and for the production of souvenirs and devotional articles popular with tourists.[35]

The more significant environment for the Arab inhabitants of nineteenth-century Palestine was the village and its surrounding fields and pasturelands. The majority of people (60 percent, excluding Jews, as late as 1948) depended on agriculture and ancillary occupations for their livelihood. Attachment to the land was therefore an economic necessity.[36] At the center of this relationship between the peasant and the land lay the village. Each village consisted of a single or several family clans, and it was to this community that the peasants gave their primary loyalties. The Ottoman sultan was the ultimate owner of most rural land, but peasants had the right to cultivate particular parcels, a right that passed down from father to son. The parcels consisted of fixed proportions of a village's surrounding fields and were distributed to each family group. Grazing lands were also held in common and all villagers had rights to gather wood, water, and other resources on village and nearby state lands. Changes in land tenure began after the Turkish government passed new laws in 1858 requiring that land be registered. The peasants, fearing taxes and army conscription, frequently registered their parcels in the names of fictitious or dead individuals, or allowed town merchants or other notables to register the land in their own names. Thus, lands once held collectively on an informal basis become the private holdings of absentee landowners, and peasants who had once held traditional rights to their lands became tenants working for others.[37]

Wheat, barley, durra, sesame, olive oil, and citrus formed the basis of nineteenth-century Palestinian agriculture. Vineyards were prominent in some areas. Farmers also grew figs, apricots, almonds, apples, melons, pomegranates, and mulberries in smaller quantities. Sheep and goats comprised an integral part of the rural economy, providing meat, milk, wool, skins, cheese, and yogurt.[38]

These and other elements of the Palestinian environment often carried meanings quite different from those perceived by Western visitors and Zionist immigrants. Travelers remarked on the poor state of agriculture in the region, but the value of crops and fruit trees for peasants reflected spiritual as well as practical considerations. Arabs believed that olives, figs, grapes, and pomegranates, important commodities in the agricultural economy, were also among the "fruits of Paradise." The times for harvesting these fruits were occasions for both hard work and joyous festivities as families left the village for several days at a time to collect the fruits from trees and vines in the nearby hills.[39]

The olive tree provided a particularly apt example of the practical, spiritual, and emotional significance which various environmental features held for the Palestinian peasantry. Peasants and townspeople alike depended on olive oil for cooking and lighting before the introduction of kerosene. It was also the basis of a thriving soap-making industry, Palestine's primary export throughout the nineteenth century. Beyond its value for subsistence, however, the villager viewed its fertility as a symbol of prosperity and good fortune. Although peasants did not own the land they tilled, they did own their individual olive trees. These trees often lived for hundreds of years, their fruits sustaining generations of the same family.[40] Today the olive tree is a potent symbol of Palestinian nationalism and resistance.

Many travelers commented on the strangeness of the window-less, flat-roofed stone and mud-brick houses they saw in Arab villages. Writers often dismissed them as crude and unappealing, "ovens," in the words of a visitor quoted earlier. Yet these dwellings, poor but adapted to the local environment, provided foci of attachment and identity for their owner. An Arab proverb, "Leave your children either a [house of] stone or [an orchard of] trees," points to the importance of the home and the olive tree. To rent a house was a disgrace. A peasant song expressed the sense of strong personal attachment felt toward the house:

O our house with reddish stones!
We have gone and others have inhabited thee,
O our house in which we grew up,
Which no longer offers us shelter nor can we be proud in thee!
O our house, if Bedouins, and not we, should take their abode
    within thee,
Receive them kindly till we return,
Then shall I bring thee, O house, two loads of indigo,
And shall adorn thee, O house, as brides are adorned.[41]

The variety of blessings and curses concerning the house indicates its central importance to the well-being of its owners. New homes were believed to be inhabited by spirits (*jinn*) whom the family needed to placate before moving in. This ceremony provided an occasion for great celebrations involving relatives, neighbors, workmen, and even passersby.[42]

The flat roof was an important center of family and village activity. During the summer months, festive gatherings took place on the roof rather than in the courtyard. On summer nights, whole families slept there under the stars to escape the heat. Women often performed daily chores on the roof where they could converse with neighbors on nearby rooftops. In some areas, when a notable person recovered from an illness, villagers set fires on the rooftops to announce the news to neighboring communities.[43]

The village provided physical and spiritual protection for its

residents. European observers often spoke critically of the confusing layout of villages and their lack of open space. The narrow
and irregular streets, typical of many preindustrial settlements,
maximized defense, however, and the layout, the outcome of
communal evolution, provided safe and enclosed spaces.[44] Local
saints also protected the villager. Each village or district had at
least one saint, or *wali,* who was responsible for the inhabitants'
welfare. The *wali's* tomb or shrine was usually located in or near
the village. At these sites, residents would leave offerings of food
or money, which were then distributed among the poor. Peasants
often stored their goods in or around the shrines in the belief that
no one would dare steal goods under the care of a *wali.* Away
from home, travelers invoked the protection of their home village's saint, often vowing to give money in return for the repair
of the saint's shrine or for distribution to the poor.[45]

Shrines and tombs were not the only sacred elements in the
landscape. Certain trees, caves, springs, streams, wells, rocks,
heaps of stones, and ruins also carried spiritual meanings. Some
assumed a sacred character by virtue of their proximity to a *wali's*
shrine, others because some extraordinary event occurred there,
and still others because local residents believed them to be inhabited by the spirits of holy men or *jinn.* Strict rules of behavior
applied in these places. If a holy tree was a fruit tree, for example,
passersby could eat as much as they pleased of its fruits but were
forbidden to carry any away.[46]

Animals and plants possessed their own intrinsic religious value
apart from that conveyed by saints or demons. Peasants believed
that God would allow animals, trees, and even stones to witness
on the day of judgment in favor of human souls. Proverbial expressions spoke of trees and crops praising God. The longitudinal
groove on grains of wheat was thought to represent the letter alif,
the first letter of God's name. The calls of certain birds were heard
as repetitions of God's attributes (for example, the dove coos: "Ya
ra'uf, ya ra'uf—O Merciful, O Merciful").[47]

The landscape of Palestine was alive with meaning and value
for its inhabitants just as it was for Western Christians and Jews.
For Palestinians, however, these meanings and values arose from
the daily personal and communal interactions of people with their

environment. Theirs was the landscape of home, not of biblical history, romantic adventure, or prophetic fulfillment. Individual houses, villages, crops, trees, springs, and even rocks possessed distinctive associations which made them special places and features in the experiential landscape of the individual and of the community. The material and spiritual lives of the people were bound up with the land in the most intimate and fundamental ways. A peasant saying expressed this relationship simply and concisely: "We cannot reach His sky; therefore we kiss the earth."[48]

LANDSCAPE AS TEXT

Geographers often speak of "reading the landscape." Traditionally, the geographer has been the reader, looking for clues in the environmental text which will explain its origin, development, and human transformation. The geographer as analyst attempts to be objective, an outsider examining an object. But individual readers also construct readings of texts, interpreting them through a framework built upon past experiences and present expectations. This chapter has presented in brief outline various readings of the Palestinian landscape of the nineteenth and early twentieth centuries. Western Christians and Zionists were outsiders looking at the land with explicit goals in mind. Their own backgrounds and hopes heavily influenced their interpretations. The Western Christian reading went hand in hand with European manipulation of the Near East and the culture of industrial capitalism. The Zionist interpretation shared certain aspects of this view, particularly in regard to the links between land, territorial possession, and nationhood, but also reflected the deep yearning of a persecuted and alienated people for a secure home. Both interpretations involved a highly conscious and intellectualized articulation of place.

Palestinians, on the other hand, were insiders largely unconcerned with articulating their relationship to their home; therefore, this relationship remained unarticulated and devoid of ideology throughout the nineteenth century. Without a defined framework for embracing and promulgating a nationally meaningful land rhetoric, Palestinian Arabs were at a disadvantage in confronting European and Zionist penetration. Only in the twentieth century, and particularly after 1948, have Palestinian literary figures articulated their sense of place within the framework of an explicitly national landscape having a generally recognized symbolic meaning.

CHAPTER 3

THE LITERATURE OF
STRUGGLE AND LOSS

1920–1960

By 1920, a number of forces had been set in motion which served to intensify the conflict between Arabs and Jews in Palestine. In particular, the Balfour Declaration of 1917, in which the British government pledged its "best endeavors to facilitate" the establishment of a Jewish "national home," gave Zionists a firmer foothold in Palestine.[1] At the same time, the end of Turkish rule increased Arab expectations of imminent national independence. French and British control after the First World War frustrated nationalist aspirations in much of the Near East, but only in Palestine were the local inhabitants threatened with actual dispossession of their lands. During this period of conflict, Arabs and Jews wrote passionately of Palestine, although in radically different ways. This chapter first examines the changing images of Palestine in Hebrew literature during the years of the British Mandate (1920–1948). This is followed by an exploration of the ways in which Palestinian Arab poets and authors invoked Palestine in response to the threat posed by Zionism. Finally, the discussion focuses on the development of a new sensibility toward the land in Palestinian literature during the decade after the birth of Israel in 1948.

PIONEERING IN ZION

If early Zionist images of Palestine were varied, they all shared the mark of outsiders envisioning a place as home. Palestine offered national territory, redemption, refuge, an agrarian utopia, or ful-fillment of biblical prophecy. All these visions were highly artic-ulated and discussed at length in Zionist circles in Europe, America, and Palestine. But for the majority of Jews, these visions remained intellectual wordplay. Micah Joseph Berdichevsky and Hayyim Nahman Bialik, perhaps the best-known modern Hebrew poet, both wrote of the hopelessness and suffering of Jewish life in *galut* (exile), but initially doubted their fellow Jews' commit-ment to establishing a vibrant Jewish culture along radically new principles in Palestine. Berdichevsky claimed that he would be a devoted Zionist "if he should see young Jews setting out barefoot to live in the land . . . rather than forever expatiating at a distance on the glorious ideal of reinvigorating Judaism by restoring Jewry to its ancient homeland." Instead, the overwhelming majority of Jews fleeing the suffocating ghettos of Eastern Europe emigrated westward to America and Western Europe.[2]

At the end of the First World War, however, a third wave of Jewish emigration to Palestine, known as the Third Aliyah, breathed new life into the vision of a socialist agrarian Jewish homeland. This early postwar period witnessed the birth of several organizations which, although short-lived, would leave a deep and enduring mark on Zionist land rhetoric. The Gdud Ha'avoda (Le-gion of Labor), founded on strict Communist principles, was ded-icated to building the roads and other infrastructure necessary for mass immigration of Jews. Members of the Hashomer Hatzair (The Young Watchman), inspired by the German youth move-ment and the philosophy of Martin Buber, preached the romantic ideals of a revolutionary youth culture and collective kibbutz life.[3] The Hehalutz (The Pioneer) organized thousands of young Jews in Europe and America for training in both socialism and farming to prepare them for life in Palestine. Based on the principles and activities of these and other groups during the 1920s and 1930s, the kibbutzim population rose from 700 in 1922 to over 25,000 by 1939.[4] Although the latter figure represented only 5 percent of the total Jewish population of Palestine, the fervor, ideals, and experiences of the young *halutzim*, or "pioneers," during this period shaped an image of the land which has remained an integral part of Israeli ideology to this day.[5]

The *halutzim*'s experience working the soil served to bring Hebrew literature in Palestine "down to earth." Israeli poet and critic Simon Halkin noted in 1950 that "just as in our own day Israel has acquired a more concrete physical meaning to the Jew than ever before in his exile, so the poetic expression of that new meaning has become more immediate, more sensory and sensuous than it ever could have been in traditional Jewish literature."[6] The new vision, deeply influenced by the *halutzim*, was no longer that of an amorphous, abstract utopia, but of a community bounded and rooted in the soil itself. Jacob Steinberg, a poet and essayist from Ukraine who settled in Palestine during this period, expressed the desire for boundedness. "We wish to descend downhill," he wrote, "where the atmosphere is heavy and mist rises from the earth, hiding distances from view."[7] On the barren heights of exile, space had no bounds and all places seemed equally meaningless. Hebrew literature during the 1920s and 1930s articulated the desire for identifiable boundaries and a defined sense of place. A poem by Levi ben Amittai demarcates a sharp border between the poet's place and the outside world:

> Now I know my boundary. The line of the furrow stretches.
> Tread on, and crush the multitudinous rocky obstacles.[8]

Simultaneously delimiting boundaries and narrowing horizons opens up new opportunities by providing a more secure foundation for the individual. This is the paradox of being at home in one's place. David Shimonovitz, a popular poet of the pioneering period and himself an immigrant, felt this paradox embodied in his Palestine-born son, who gave little thought to anything beyond his immediate ken. In "Dewdrops at Night," Shimonovitz writes of Jewish children born in Palestine:

> They lack the depth achieved by children of affliction
> only . . .[9]

Yet it is these children, the poet believes, who will be the true inheritors of the land, because they know it and love it for itself rather than for its symbols. Shimonovitz watches his son working in the fields and henhouse and exploring nearby caves, apparently fearless and familiar with every tree and hillock. The boy's light-minded work and play in this landscape represents for his anguished father a continuity with ancient Hebrews. These children can take up their place in the land unself-consciously, without knowing the fear and rootlessness which previous generations experienced in the Diaspora. In their bounded relation with the land, the past merges with a promising future.

The "earthy exhilaration" and "intoxication with nature" so characteristic of Hebrew literature during the 1920s and 1930s is not, however, an evocation of the land as Zionists originally encountered it.[10] It celebrates, rather, the transformation of the old Palestine and the creation of a new land which expresses the new Jewish spirit. Abraham Schlonsky, another poet of the *halutz* generation, paints a landscape which, through the creative labors of young pioneers, transforms and transcends the traditional elements of Judaic ritual. "New homes stand forth as do phylacteries," he writes, and Jewish-built highways glide through the land "like phylactery-bands."[11]

Through these acts of labor, the *halutzim* wished to transform from words into reality a bond that did not have to be articulated, justified, or explained. In the active creation of an intimate link between soil and people, the *halutzim* sought to destroy the persistent, invasive self-consciousness which Halkin called "the most baneful connotation of Jewishness in the modern world."[12]

The irony is that, as with many nationalist endeavors, this search for rootedness had to be highly self-conscious, aggressively pursued, and continuously communicated to fresh waves of immigrants. The newcomers, with no knowledge of their new home, had to be taught to be natives. Eventually *yedi'at haaretz*, "knowledge of the land," became an integral part of kibbutz life and school curricula. It incorporated geography, natural history, geology, and archaeology, combining them with nature hikes, camping, and paramilitary training. Meron Benvenisti, whose father was one of the proponents of *yedi'at haaretz*, notes that the biblical meaning of *yedi'a* relates to sexual knowledge of a woman, so that knowledge of the land equates with physical possession. By walking the land, identifying historic sites, and listing plants and animals, young Zionists staked their claim to territory and identity. By increasing topographic knowledge and physical endurance, *yedi'at haaretz* also served strategic and military ends.[13] The celebration of nature and the pioneering experience articulated the relation of the "new Jew" to the land and became an important rhetorical weapon in the struggle to establish Israel. The imagery from this pioneering period continues to buttress the contemporary Israeli sense of identity, although 90 percent of Israeli Jews live in urban places.[14]

For young Zionists engaged in knowing the land, Arabs provided convenient illustrations of primitive bonds between people and place. "The Arab," wrote Moshe Shamir of his childhood days in Palestine in the 1920s, "lived in the Jewish consciousness as a symbol of naturalness, of deep-rootedness."[15] Shamir recounts learning "from the Arab how to wash and drink like a child of nature" and then goes on to describe the animal-like movements of "the Arab," performing his ablutions before prayer using only sand and a scant amount of water. Shamir and his young friends prided themselves on being able to mimic these native rituals.[16] Benvenisti likewise recalls envying the seemingly innate navigational skills of the Bedouins. When leading youth groups on desert nature hikes, he would hide behind a rock to read his map, embarrassed that he still needed such an artificial aid.[17]

The darker side of the Arab as embodiment of nature is the Arab as irrational, uncivilized, and consumed by an impulsive, violent temper. The conflation of the pioneer, *yedi'at haaretz*, peaceful Arab as a child of nature, and violent Arab as a would-be murderer is manifested in a remarkable passage by Moshe Shamir in his book, *My Life with Ishmael*.[18] Shamir recounts taking part in field exercises on his kibbutz as a young man. As he surveyed the hills of Ein Hashofet, "the world looked like a topographical map brought to life, a field of maneuvers and action," Shamir writes. "The ruin, deserted Khan—a target, an enemy position. The wadi—'dead' ground beyond firing range." He goes on to detail how his unit lay positioned, ready to ambush the phantom enemy, who is, of course, "the Arab." Meanwhile, ignoring all this youthful commotion around him, an Arab shepherd tends his small flock of sheep. Shamir continues:

> Lying there in ambush. . . . Watching. I watch the shepherd. It's impossible not to—for we could hear him too. I have never in my life heard a concert like that. I have never had such a profound sense of contact with the most primeval syllables of existence. He was talking to his flock; he held them in his hand—without stirring from his place. Standing there, one foot on the ground, the other curled around his staff, both hands resting on top of it, one above the other. . . . He didn't wave his staff, he threw no stones, he had no sheepdog. Only talking to them, uninterrupted talk. There are no letters for the sounds he made, there is no way of writing those syllables down. Just to close your eyes and feel the absolute stillness in your heart . . . to hear that moment again.[19]

Ironically, Shamir recalls this event only to profess his respect for "the ordinary Arab" (in contrast to educated, urban Arabs, whom he blames for years of conflict and hostility) and to portray himself as free of ethnic bias. It is a nostalgic and reassuring vision of simplicity. The Arab shepherd communes in a wordless primal language with his sheep, careful not to get in the way of the young pioneers as they bond with their ancient homeland and practice for war. Yet the idea of the land transformed into a topographic map constitutes a profound negation of rootedness. The map is a carefully crafted strategic tool, a means of navigation and possession for those coming to the land from outside. The shepherd would probably make no sense of it. His links to the land—naive, unself-conscious, and resistant to capture by the written word— embodied the ideal of rootedness for pioneering Zionists, an ideal they could not achieve. But it is the shepherd who will lose. His wordlessness, his inability to converse in the language of power and possession, will fail him in his confrontation with a highly wrought rhetoric of place and identity.

EARLY PALESTINIAN LITERATURE AND
THE RESPONSE TO ZIONISM

If the experience of farming in Palestine lent to Hebrew literature a new, more tangible, direct, and passionate feeling for the land, we might expect an equally if not more intense image in the literature of the Palestinian Arabs who had been working the soil for generations. Yet no such image appears in Palestinian literature during the Mandate period. There is little description of landscape or evocation of a sense of personal, individual attachment to particular places, even though Palestinian writers clearly recognized the growing threat posed by Zionism. One reason for this absence was the social background of Palestinian literary figures at the time. They were a small group, for the most part the sons of wealthy and influential families, educated outside Palestine and with few immediate ties to the land. They viewed the British Mandate and Zionism as a two-pronged imperialist threat from the West. Their response was to raise the banner of pan-Arab nationalism and to stress the political and economic aspects of the struggle. This response came primarily in the form of poetry written for public occasions.

Poetry is one of the most respected Arab art forms, and in it Arab culture finds its most public and characteristic expression. Poetry's classical role included recording the glories of one's own people and dispiriting the adversary. After falling into eclipse under centuries of Ottoman Turkish rule, classical Arab poetry experienced a renaissance with the rise of Arab nationalism in the late nineteenth and early twentieth centuries. Returning to their golden past, Arab nationalists found in classical poetry an appropriate vehicle for promulgating the concept of pan-Arabism. Almost without exception, Palestinian poets of this period resorted to these traditional poetic forms when writing of their homeland's struggle to inspire a populace familiar with classical poetry's tone and signals.[20] The reservoir of classical Arab motifs, metaphors, and symbols, however, did not emphasize a personal and emotional relationship between the individual and the local environment.

This is not to say that nature imagery is absent in traditional

Arab poetry. Pre-Islamic poetry abounds in images of nature. In later urban Islamic society, however, this imagery becomes highly stylized. Nature symbols in classical poetry are simple and concrete. A crescent moon, for example, might represent the image of a boat.[21] A poem written by a priest in Nazareth prior to the First World War typifies this representation of landscape:

> From the valley of Jezreel a city is beheld
> Crowding the clouds of the sky in claiming glory.
> It mounts the slopes of the mountains and looks down over their
>   valleys, the sea, the Jordan and the highlands beyond,
> A queen of beauty sitting on a throne,
> her goodness appearing near and far,
> Now she turns toward Tabor,* now to Carmel,*
> heedless of the tides,
> She gazes at Hermon,* delighting in his white head,
> And Gilboa,* overwhelmed, adores her.[22]

The poet invokes pleasing landscape features but expresses no relation between people and nature and no sense of the place of people in the landscape. This particular poem appeared before the upheavals caused by the Balfour Declaration and lacks political content. Although later nationalist poetry sensed the threat to the homeland, its treatment of place and environment is similar.

Perhaps most important to note is that the nineteenth- and early twentieth-century European glorification of folk culture and the concatenation of blood and soil had no direct counterpart in Arab society during the initial encounter with Zionism. Several authors have noted the influence of the German youth movement and its obsession with nature and folk on the culture of Zionism. This was the Western *zeitgeist*, which was eventually played out with horrific consequences. That Arab intellectuals and town-dwellers did not speak in the same terms, that there were no Arab youth groups redeeming their people's soil and no glorification of Arab peasants, appeared to Zionists as evidence that Arab elites

---

*Names of mountains visible from Nazareth.

cared little for their land or their people. But Arab writers were couching their ideas and experiences in a different rhetoric, well established in their own culture, which came to face a fundamental challenge in the encounter with Zionism.

THE POETRY OF CONFLICT: 1920–1948

Poetry was the preferred vehicle in Palestine for expressing nationalist sentiment, and during the period between 1920 and 1948, both literary figures and political leaders viewed the struggle with Zionism and the British Mandate within a nationalist framework. Poets intended their works to be read at public and religious gatherings; at meetings of literary, cultural, religious, and social clubs; at political demonstrations; and at public funerals of Arabs killed in riots or executed by the British. Novels and short stories, on the other hand, were recent innovations and were not widely read. The few works of this kind that did appear during this period dealt mostly with the individual's role in society and did not treat the issue of the land and its usurpation in depth.[23]

Palestinian poets employed a variety of Arabic terms to invoke the land. *Bilad* (country), *watan* (homeland), *mawtin* (native place), *tharan* (ground, soil), *ard* (earth, land), and *turab* (dust, dirt) were among the most common. The essential meanings of these words are specific and concrete, expressing distinctive human places and elements of the tangible environment. Poets, however, employed them in a generic sense to inspire a feeling of national belonging. In doing so they removed these expressions from the realm of personal experience and increased the figurative distance between the actual land as earth and its rhetorical representation as nation. *Mawtin*, for example, no longer referred to the place where an individual dwelled but to the homeland in a general sense. The land entered the realm of rhetorical abstraction, where it could be poetically enriched by the blood of martyred sons or despoiled by ruthless enemies.

Yet Palestinian poets of this period were not simply engaging in nationalist sloganeering. They dealt with many of the concrete issues of the day and performed an important role in informing the general public about events and processes which were certain to affect them. These included the activities of the British authorities, the policies of other Arab countries, increasing Jewish immigration, and the Zionist acquisition of Arab land, plus demonstrations, strikes, and other forms of resistance. Poets were perhaps the most critical of their own class. The foremost Palestinian poet of the 1930s, Ibrahim Tuqan, bitterly attacked the complacency he saw around him:

> You—I know you well—care only for trivial, empty appearances.
> Those around you sense your fate, and the news of it has spread to
> distant lands. Mighty palaces will not remain to their inhabitants,
> nor narrow huts.[24]

Wealthy Arab landowners who sold their land to Zionists were Tuqan's primary villains. The selling of land was both an affront to Arab nationalists, who saw their aspirations for independence foiled by the Zionists, and a tragedy for peasants. The latter rarely owned land themselves; instead they worked as tenant farmers for absentee owners. When Zionists bought the land and insisted on using only Jewish labor, Arab farmers lost their source of livelihood and gained nothing on the sale. Tuqan attacked the sellers of land, who were already the wealthiest men in the land, for betraying their country in return for more money:

> As for those who sell the country, they are a gang
> Whose continued existence is a disgrace to the homeland . . .
> And they are, despite all, its leaders and protectors!!
> By their hands it shall be ruined,
> Bought and sold by their hands.[25]

Burhan al-Din al-ʿAbushi's "The Sad Valley" addressed the same problem specifically in the Marj ibn ʿAmr region of north central Palestine:

> The Arabs have sold your dignity, O Valley of Ibn ʿAmr:
> The children of the West are like the offspring of a lioness

While the children of the East seize each other's throat. . . .
Janin, Zarʿin, and Beith-Shean are in danger
And Wasilat al Dahr in confusion,
Exile is awaiting at the gate—
So strangers are warning us
As they wait lustfully watching us.[26]

Many poets clearly foresaw the possibility of losing the land, but they put their fears and warnings into a nationalist framework rather than a personal one. While al-ʾAbushi mentions specific localities, for example, the symbolism remains straightforward and political. Wild beasts from the West wait to devour Palestine while her Arab siblings fight among themselves.

Other places and features appeared in the poetry of this period in similar ways. Many poems featured Jerusalem and its holy sites, including al-Aqsa Mosque, al-Buraq, the Dome of the Rock, and the Church of the Holy Sepulchre.[27] Jerusalem figured politically because of its status as the headquarters of the British Mandate.[28] Its greater significance, however, lay in the symbolic importance of its Christian and Muslim holy sites, which poets invoked to inspire resistance to the "new Crusaders," both British and Zionist. ʿAbd al-Rahim Mahmud, a poet active in the resistance who died in the 1948 war, gained immediate fame when he addressed the following verses to the then Saudi prince Saʿud ibn ʿAbd al-ʾAziz, during the latter's visit to Jerusalem in 1935:

The Aqsa Mosque, oh Prince, have you come to pay reverence to
    it,
Or to bid it farewell before it is lost,
A sanctuary to be ravaged by every mutilated runaway slave,
by every roving vagabond?
And tomorrow, how near it is! For us nothing will remain but
remorse and flowing tears.[29]

Al-ʾAbushi appealed to the leaders of Iraq to come to the aid of Palestine by arguing that all Arabs must be liberated before any of them could be truly free. He invoked al-Buraq to inspire Muslim pride:

> The independence of the Tigris land shall not be secured
> Before all of Arabdom's children are gathered to the flag.
> Only then shall I see above al-Buraq high and mighty
> The Iraqi flag waving proudly.[30]

Many of the poets were Christians and they, to an even greater extent than their Muslim compatriots, took care to present symbols which would appeal to adherents of both religions. Perceptive Palestinian leaders strove to present a united front to the British authorities and to the Zionists. Wadi' al-Bustani, a Lebanese Christian, came to Palestine as an official in the Mandate Administration but quickly became a major figure in the nationalist movement and one of its most prolific poets. He repeatedly spoke of Jerusalem as a city holy to both Christianity and Islam, and he often invoked al-Aqsa Mosque, al-Buraq, the Church of the Holy Sepulchre, the Dome of the Rock, and the Mount of Olives as national religious sites threatened by foreigners.[31]

As the struggle against foreign forces intensified, poets employed the traditional technique of referring to previous Arab victories to inspire the public. Few of these successes had taken place on Palestinian soil. One exception was the Battle of Hittin in the Galilee, in which Salah al-Din (known in the West as Saladin) decisively defeated a Crusader army, paving the way for the Muslim reconquest of Jerusalem. Hittin became a potent symbol of Palestinian Arab resistance and is mentioned in several poems of the period.[32] For the most part, however, historic references are to other lands, further removing poetry from the land it was attempting to save. As the specter of defeat loomed larger, several poets conjured up the image of Muslim Spain, a golden period and place in Arab history until Christian conquerors forced its Muslim inhabitants into exile.[33] The anticipation of Palestine's loss thus appears in poetry as a loss for the Arab nation as a whole in national political, social, and economic terms rather than as a personal loss in emotional terms.

NOVELS AND SHORT STORIES

Novels and short stories played a marginal role in expressing relations between Palestinians and Zionists before 1948. These were new genres for the Arab world, and literary figures perceived them as more suitable for exploring the individual's inner world than for treating issues of public concern. Moreover, the audience for prose writing was extremely restricted, existing almost entirely among the educated elite.[34]

While its concern for lived experience might have made prose writing a more effective medium for evoking feelings for the land, much of this writing dealt only with the new social challenges facing Arab society, specifically those involving urban upper classes. An early novel by Jabra Ibrahim Jabra, written in 1946, portrays the individual's alienation in a cold, anonymous city.[35] A 1947 novel by Iskandir Khuri al-Baytjalli, author of several nationalist anthems and fiery political poems, deals exclusively with marriage and sexual relations.[36] Stories which deal with Zionism often focus on the corrupting influences of Jewish immigrants. In one of her short stories, Najwa Qaʿwar portrays a struggle between good and evil, with Arab village girls representing the former and loose-living blond immigrant girls the latter.[37] Musa al-Husayni, on the other hand, depicts the homeland's potential loss through the vehicle of an animal fable in which a mother hen, faced with uninvited guests in the chicken house, counsels her family to relinquish their home to the strangers. The story created a controversy because it was unclear whether al-Husayni was praising traditional Arab hospitality or ridiculing Arab political leadership.[38]

A few prose examples of environmental imagery exist which address a more specific sense of place, prefiguring motifs which would become more common after 1948. In a short story entitled "The Sad Sisters," Najati Sidqi relates the history of five sycamore trees standing in a row along a Tel Aviv street. The area, previously an Arab-owned orchard on the outskirts of Jaffa, has fallen victim to the increasing sprawl of Jewish-built Tel Aviv. Buildings, cafés, and clubs now surround the trees. While resting at the foot of one of the sycamores, the narrator dreams that they are five sisters, dressed in the black clothes of mourning. In voices hoarse from weeping, the sisters each recount what they have seen taking place in their shade. They remember lovers exchanging vows, Sufi mystics debating religious points, the founding and expansion of Tel Aviv, and the imposition of British rule, including the hanging of Arab martyrs from their branches. The youngest sister, born in 1917, has no recollection of an Arab past in this place but senses the grief of her older sisters. As the narrator awakes, stormy autumn winds are roaring through the street, "but they had no strength against those trees; they remained as firmly fixed as a towering mountain."[39]

Another instance of a more personal expression of attachment to place is found in Asma Tubi's collection of reflections, *Talks from the Heart*. At one point she writes of her uncle working the soil in their garden, his sweat dripping down and mingling with the dirt. "I heard him whisper: How right this is! The sweat of my forehead and the strength of my muscles lie in this ground. The blood of my heart is there, too. My forefathers worked it for decades. I will not be the man to lose it."[40]

This image of an individual working a particular parcel of land and becoming one with its soil rarely occurred in Palestinian literature before 1948. The transformation of a place and its meaning on a personal, experiential plane, as portrayed in "The Sad Sisters," was equally rare. Most Palestinian authors in this period expressed their feelings about their home within traditional political and social frameworks. Confined to these frameworks, the rhetoric which authors employed distanced their works from the actual landscape and from the lived experience of its inhabitants. This is not to say that this literature, poetry in particular, did not speak to the people. By most accounts, it succeeded in warning and inspiring the populace, which was its aim. But it did not express an experiential sense of place, that is, of belonging to a particular and well-defined environment. Nor did it express a sense of what role the land played in the lives of its residents, or of the deep and powerful effects its potential loss would have. These issues remained for the most part in the realm of everyday life and folklore.

If Hebrew literature from the 1920s to 1948 came down from the heights to embrace "new Jews" in their new land and home,

Palestinian literature must be regarded as inhabiting the skies, observing clearly the larger political picture but missing the human details in the landscape. Literature began to reveal some of these details after 1948, when a large number of Palestinians suddenly found themselves literally on the outside looking in.

THE LITERATURE OF THE LOST LAND: 1948–1960

Israel was declared a state on May 14, 1948. During the rest of that spring and summer, war and attacks on civilians forced between 500,000 and 800,000 Palestinians, 40 to 60 percent of the total Arab population, from their homes into what many assumed and prayed would be only temporary exile. Another 120,000 people in the Gaza Strip and in border villages of the West Bank lost their sources of livelihood.[41] Among the exiles were most of the urban intelligentsia, including the active literary figures. Within the new Israel, conditions did not favor literary creativity. Most of the Palestinians who remained in the country lived in rural areas where educational opportunities were limited. Contact with literary currents in the Arab world and beyond grew difficult, censorship was strict, and Israeli political parties largely controlled the few publishing presses available to Arabs.[42] Little in the way of independent Palestinian literature appeared in Israel until the late 1950s. Poets and novelists in exile, however, continued to practice their crafts, and in their works a new sensitivity toward the land first emerges.

Despite the pan-nationalist rhetoric calling for one great Arab nation, Palestinians in exile quickly realized that they were Palestinians first and foremost, with no political authority to protect their interests, and alternately used and abused by Arab governments. While nationalist poetry still thrived, it took on new forms and subjects. Classical forms of poetry no longer provided an adequate framework for expressing the new situation. Palestinian poet and critic Jabra Ibrahim Jabra comments that after 1948, as the Arab world "embarked upon a new phase in the search for its identity and sources of strength, the poet's stance was one of intense consciousness of self."[43] Palestinian poets turned toward their own experience and that of their compatriots. With the future uncertain, they first looked toward the past. Nostalgia became the most characteristic element in the image of Palestine in exile literature during the 1950s. Rather than invoking past Arab glories, holy places, or nationalist ideals, exiled poets wrote of scenes from their youth. It is in these scenes that a sense of attachment to the land begins to emerge and in which the land's specific qualities find a voice.

The nostalgic perspective of much of this work romanticized the land as a lost paradise. Jabra's "In the Deserts of Exile" conjured up this lost landscape:

> Our Palestine, green land of ours;
> Its flowers as if embroidered on women's gowns;
> March adorns its hills
> With the jewel-like peony and narcissus;
> April bursts open in its plains
> With flowers and bride-like blossoms;
> May is our rustic song
> Which we sing at noon,
> In the blue shadows,
> Among the olive trees of our valleys,
> and in the ripeness of the fields
> We wait for the promise of July
> And the joyous dance amidst the harvest.
> O land of ours where our childhood passed
> Like dreams in the shade of the orange grove,
> Among the almond trees in the valleys.[44]

Here we find emerging, albeit in a highly idealized version, landscape features of daily rural life. It is, to a limited extent, a literary interpretation of the life of rural Palestine before the disruptions of the twentieth century. It invokes flowers, seasons, embroidery patterns on women's dresses, olive and almond trees, and harvest festivities, all elements of a way of life which suddenly loomed large in the thoughts of the exiled poet.

Fadwa Tuqan, a West Bank poet and the younger sister of Ibrahim Tuqan, employed all the faculties of sense in describing the experience of a refugee determined to return to the fields that he once tilled. Leaving a camp on the West Bank by night, the refugee makes his way toward his home in a dreamlike trance. The lights of Jaffa sparkle in the distance and he thinks he can hear the surf rolling onto the seashore. The scent of oranges envelops him. Unsure of where to go, he hears the nurturing earth calling to him. With an outpouring of emotion, he arrives at his destination:

> He fell down on his land, excitedly taking in
> the smell of its moist soil,
> He clung to its trees and embraced its stones,
> Rolling his cheeks and mouth in its wide bosom
> He threw onto it all the weight of years of pain.[45]

A few steps away Israeli sentries catch sight of him and shoot him dead, a fate believed to be shared by many Palestinians who attempted to infiltrate back into their villages in Israel after the 1948 war. This sensual unification with the land becomes an increasingly popular motif in Palestinian literature during the 1950s. No longer is the object of attachment an abstract homeland but a mothering earth of soil, trees, and stone. The Palestinian poet yearns for a defined place, its boundaries clear and its distances hidden.

Post-1948 literature abounds with images of precisely delineated and bounded environmental features like the house and garden. These represent places of attachment and meaning in daily life. Harun Hashim Rashid, for example, wrote a poem in 1957 about his former house in Gaza:

> Our house in Zaytun [Olive] Quarter . . .
> Lying at the edge . . . with the goldfinch
> On the branch of the almond tree, and the lemon tree . . .
> You stir my sorrows,
> You are a piece of me and of my years.[46]

The house and garden also provided the main characters for ʿIsa al-Naʿuri's 1959 novel, *House Beyond the Borders*. The house is the home of a Jaffa family with two young boys. A third child, who died, is buried in the garden, giving it added emotional significance. The novel relates the idyllic life of the two boys, using innumerable adjectives of sweetness, beauty, and happiness. Al-Na'uri then turns to the nightmare of their exile and their longing to return. In a melodramatic ending, the youngest brother sneaks back across the border and reaches the garden, only to be gunned down by an Israeli. The story, as Palestinian critic 'Abd al-Karim al-Ashtar points out, is too simple and superficial to be of artistic merit, but it is indicative of the types of landscape features which took on new meaning after 1948.[47]

Poets also invoked their hometowns, again equating their past with a particular place. Some poems, like Ahmad Fahmi's paean to his native Safed, employ simple, external imagery in the classical tradition:

> Sons of the fatherland!
> Do you remember our homes in Safed?
> Do you remember its dreamy days,
> Its majestic Jarmaq,
> The morning in the heights of Galilee,
> The happiness of the days at Dair al-Asad?[48]

Harun Hashim Rashid wrote of Jaffa in a more personal way. In "Among the Strangers," a girl repeatedly inquires of her father why they are living away from their home in Jaffa:

> Will we go to Jaffa . . .
> Shall I enter my room, tell me,
> Shall I enter it with my dreams,
> Will I meet it and it meet me,
> Will it hear the sounds of my footsteps?[49]

Jaffa appears perhaps more frequently in the prose and poetry of the post-1948 period than any other Palestinian town. Its literary preeminence eclipses even Jerusalem, although the latter remains to this day a central symbol in the political struggle. Mahmud al-Hut typifies this bond with Jaffa, his native city:

> Jaffa! My tears have dried but I still wail,
> Will I ever see you again?
> My memory of you is fresh,
> Living within my innermost soul. . . .
> What ails my heart? Wherever I turn it sadly cries
> For my own native town.[50]

Why does Jaffa figure so prominently? It was a port of some importance in pre-Zionist Palestine. It is still remembered for its orange groves, which gave the town a picture-postcard appearance before Tel Aviv's expansion engulfed it. The establishment of Tel Aviv early in this century made Jaffa one of the first places in Palestine to feel the Zionist threat. Under Israeli control, it is now a chic district of Tel Aviv. But Jaffa was also visible to refugees on the West Bank. Raja Shehadeh, a Palestinian lawyer who grew up in a refugee family on the West Bank, writes of the romantic picture he drew of Jaffa as a boy watching its distant lights at night.[51] It was a Palestinian city which refugees could see but to which they could not return, a symbol of an idyllic past lying just beyond reach. The town's clear visibility made the sense of loss all the more gnawing and poignant. Kamal Nasir, gazing toward Jaffa, expresses this pain and frustration together with the emotional exhaustion they create:

> Wounded shore! Vainly fluttering before my eyes!
> You are ever in my heart. . . .
> My hands outstretched to you
> Fall wearily beneath the weight of longing.[52]

This stance of the exiled author looking toward home aptly describes the position of Palestinian literature vis-à-vis the land in the decade following 1948. Poets and novelists turned their attention to the personal meanings which the land held for them. They stressed the importance of particular places and articulated the attachment they felt for the physical landscape rather than for an abstract political entity. Yet they found themselves outside its borders, lost in a limitless exile. Just as the establishment of boundaries and form led to a blossoming of life and opportunity for Jews in Palestine, so the destruction of these same features in the Palestinian landscape led to a restriction of hope and an overwhelming sense of oppression. Mahmud al-Hut succinctly expresses this sense of oppressive restriction:

> Lost paradise! You were never too small for us,
> But now vast countries are indeed too small.
> Torn asunder your people,
> Wandering under every star.[53]

Although Palestinian literature in the years immediately following 1948 presents a more detailed picture of the Palestinian landscape and its significant places and features than earlier works, its representations lack dimension. It is largely a landscape of yearning, nostalgia, and absence, expressed in simple, unambiguous images from an idealized past. This type of nostalgic vision is reminiscent of pre-Islamic poetry, in which it was common to portray a wandering nomad coming across the vestiges of an abandoned camp that bring back memories of earlier triumphs. Nostalgia such as this, however, is essentially an aesthetic response to loss. Exile literature in the decade after 1948 likewise responded aesthetically to the Palestinian tragedy. This literature showed little comprehension of the complexities of Palestine's transformation into Israel or of the new landscapes in the making. A new generation, emerging from a different social background and growing up in exile or under occupation, waited to give voice to the more subtle and complex relations between Palestinians and their land.

CHAPTER 4

LANDSCAPES OF EXILE

The immediate literary reaction to exile was to invoke nostalgic images of the lost Palestine, images which helped them to maintain a link with home under arduous circumstances. As Palestinian literature matured, however, it began to explore the environment and meaning of exile. In doing so, it has defined the antithesis of Palestine as represented by *al-ghurbah*, an Arabic term sometimes equated with *diaspora* but meaning specifically the experience of being a stranger separated from one's familiar home. This chapter examines the new settings in which displaced Palestinians found themselves and explores the environments of exile that have acquired symbolic form and content in poetry and prose.

THE SETTING OF EXILE

The violence surrounding the establishment of Israel in 1948 displaced a large segment of the Palestinian Arab population. Many fled to the area known today as the West Bank of the Jordan River, a part of Mandate Palestine which remained in Arab hands until 1967. Others crossed to the East Bank, part of Transjordan. In 1950, the West Bank was officially united with Transjordan to form the Hashemite Kingdom of Jordan. Many Arab residents of northern Palestine took refuge in Lebanon and Syria, while others in the south congregated in the Gaza area, which came under Egyptian control. By 1970, the total Palestinian population numbered about three million. Approximately 400,000 still lived within the 1948 borders of Israel. A further 600,000 lived in the West Bank and 350,000 in the Gaza Strip, both of which came under Israeli occupation in 1967. Between 800,000 and 850,000 Palestinians resided in Jordan, east of the Jordan River; 600,000 in Lebanon and Syria; and 200,000 scattered throughout the remainder of the Arab world, with much smaller numbers in Europe and the Americas.[1]

The physical settings in which displaced Palestinians found themselves often contrasted markedly with the lands left behind. Palestine comprises a mosaic of landscapes and physiographic diversity within its small area. Traveling eastward from the Mediterranean, one first passes through the coastal plain, where alluvial soils and adequate water resources provide conditions favorable to agriculture, particularly citrus cultivation. The mountains and hills of Galilee and the West Bank separate the coastal plain from the rift valley to the east. Galilee is the wettest region of Palestine, receiving in some places over 1,000 millimeters of precipitation annually, as well as having many springs and streams. It once supported the bulk of the rural population of Palestine.

The northern portion of the West Bank (referred to as Samaria by the Israelis) is less endowed with water resources than Galilee but still supports numerous Arab villages. The southern zone (called Judaea by the Israelis) is the driest of the hill regions; it is rocky and bleak, with a much smaller population. East of these hills lies the valley of the River Jordan. It includes both desert wastelands and lush oases as well as three lakes—the former Lake Hula, an extensive wetland drained by the Israelis and presently an area of fertile farmland; Lake Tiberias, the biblical Sea of Galilee; and the Dead Sea, into which the Jordan flows. The river's floodplain once boasted thick vegetation but is now mostly cleared. The climate of Palestine varies with its terrain, ranging from subalpine and temperate to Mediterranean and tropical.[2]

Displaced Palestinians from the coastal towns and plains and from Galilee who poured into the West Bank and Jordan entered a different and harsher physical environment. Much of the West

Bank is dry and rugged compared to the lands left behind. East of the Jordan River the land rises through a series of heavily dissected escarpments to a plateau which merges with the Syrian Desert. It was the social environment, however, which presented the greatest challenge. With cultivable land on the East and West Banks already scarce and with few resources of their own, refugees had to either live with relatives, move into refugee camps, or try their luck in the towns. The East Bank cities Amman and nearby Zarqa are Jordan's major industrial centers and attracted many Palestinians, although unemployment and underemployment were and remain rampant. Beirut, a flourishing center of international commerce in the 1950s and 1960s, likewise became a magnet for stateless refugees. Those with education and skills had the potential to earn a reasonable living, but urban life was harsh for the large number who came from lower-class and rural backgrounds.

The United Nations Relief and Works Agency (UNRWA) and various Arab governments established refugee camps on both the West and East Banks and in the Gaza Strip, Lebanon, and Syria, usually in arid wastelands or on city outskirts. As their temporary displaced status turned into indefinite exile, many Palestinians sought work in the Arab states bordering the Persian Gulf, where the developing oil industry provided abundant employment and higher wages. Those who had the means pursued university training and business opportunities in Europe and the Americas. But whatever the individual response, family and communal ties came under stress as traditional Palestinian society disintegrated.

These then are the "objective" settings of exile. They include the arid, rocky environments of the East and West Banks, refugee camps, crowded Arab capitals, dry and faceless desert boomtowns in the Gulf, and distant foreign cities. They also form the literary landscapes of exile which have taken on symbolic meaning in the years since 1948. Three symbolic landscapes of exile stand out in Palestinian literature: the desert, the city, and the refugee camp. While they are based on actual locales and situations, in symbolic form they embody the subjective experience of exile even more than they do the physical reality. The literary representation of these landscapes stresses the "outsideness" of *al-ghurbah* and clearly distinguishes it from the "insideness" of home.

THE DESERT

The desert, with its vast and timeless quality, is a potent symbol of *al-ghurbah*. Palestinian poets often employ it in a generic sense; that is, they refer to the desert as a generalized environment rather than as a particular place. One song laments:

> I am a friendless wanderer in the deserts,
> Behind the wires of injustice is my home.[3]

The desert was a dominant motif in the pre-Islamic poetry of Arabia and its use in Palestinian literature is no doubt influenced by these older images. But the desert of exile for the Palestinian is in no way romantic. It is a void, a nonplace in which the exile exists but feels nothing of the present. The exile's thoughts revolve around the land and life left behind. Jabra Ibrahim Jabra expresses this emptiness and yearning in a poem entitled "In the Deserts of Exile":

> Spring after spring
> In the deserts of exile
> What are we doing with our love,
> When our eyes are full of frost and death?

Rather than answering the question by addressing his present condition, Jabra launches into a nostalgic reminiscence of an idealized Palestine of flowers, olive trees, fields, and harvests. He then implores the land to

> Remember us now wandering
> Among the thorns of the desert,
> Wandering in rocky mountains.

The Zionists, he writes, have

> crushed the flowers on the hills around us,
> Destroyed the houses over our heads,
> Scattered our torn remains,
> Then unfolded the desert before us,
> With valleys writhing in hunger
> And blue shadows shattered into red thorns
> Bent over corpses left as prey for falcon and crow.

The poet concludes:

> Our land is an emerald,
> But in the deserts of exile,
> Spring after spring,
> Only the dust hisses in our face.
> What then are we doing with our love
> When our eyes and our mouth are full of frost and death?[4]

Jabra uses three different words in this poem to invoke the desert. *Bawadin*, in the title, refers to deserts or steppes. The other two words, however, imply more than the mere physical environment. *Qifar* connotes emptiness, bleak desolation, and uninhabited wastelands. *Falah* can mean waterless desert but also refers to open country or open space in general. Thus the line "Then unfolded the desert before us" also conveys in Arabic the sense of unfolding an open, endless space. The houses, fields, trees, and hills that bounded and defined the landscape of home have all vanished.

Although these desert images derive in part from the arid lands in which many Palestinian exiles found themselves, they represent not so much a real desert as a symbol of want, insecurity, emptiness, and death. These is no color or substance in this landscape, no meaning beyond pain and exhaustion. Jabra reserves colors and details for his description of Palestine. There life exists; in the desert nothing exists but frost and dust. The landscape of home abounds in images of fertility and prosperity, images which define Palestine as an object of yearning. Jabra contrasts this with the landscape of exile, a space outside of time and place, empty of both memory and hope.

Other poets use desert imagery in similar ways to express the emptiness of life after the loss of Palestine. 'Abd al-Latif 'Aql, a West Bank poet, uses the desert metaphor in a poem to his lover, who personifies Palestine:

> Perhaps the warmth in your eyes, my lady,
> Will spread shade in my house sapped by the heat of death,
> Scattering water and green grass in the desert of my barren
> room.[5]

The adjective modifying "room" in the last line is difficult to translate without losing its subtlety. The Arabic word, *jarda'*, means barren, bleak, and without vegetation but can also refer to open, unprotected borders. Again we find the sense of unbounded space. It is a figurative desert of emptiness rather than a real setting. Fadwa Tuqan also invokes the desert in this way. In her poem, "To the Face Lost in the Trackless Wilderness," the desert is a metaphor representing the barrenness of her own emotions. In this wasteland she is no longer able to grow and flourish as a loving person:

> Ah, don't fill your cards for me
> With the fragrance of remembrance or bouquets of wishes.
> Between my heart and the luxuries of love lies a desert—
> Its rays of dry summer heat twist
> Like vipers around me
> Choking the flower as they spit poison and flame.[6]

For these poets the desert symbolizes existential alienation, much as it does in modern Western literature. It may or may not be the actual environment in which they work and live. While it expresses their feelings as Palestinians, the desert as a metaphor for alienation and despair does not describe a uniquely Palestinian experience. It is also the existential dilemma of modern society, homeless in a world that appears strange and incoherent.

The desert is also a physical reality for many exiled from Palestine, however, and their experience of it differs substantially from that of others who live, work, or travel there. For the Bedouin, the desert is home; for the oil company employee, its resources promise large profits and high salaries; for the tourist, it is an exotic playground of adventure and romance. But for many Palestinians, it is a strange and hostile way station in a life that holds out no promise of a safe and final destination. Several writers speak of the hardships of exile in the desert with its particular qualities of sand, dust, drought, lack of shade, and extremes of burning heat and chilling cold. Nowhere does this real desert merge with the symbolic desert to greater effect than in the works of Ghassan Kanafani.

Kanafani was born in Acre in 1936. In 1948 he fled with his family first to Beirut and then to Damascus. In 1955, after teaching in UNRWA schools in Damascus, he moved to Kuwait, where he taught for five years. Back in Beirut again, he worked as a journalist and eventually became editor-in-chief of *al-Hadaf*, a weekly publication of the Popular Front for the Liberation of Palestine, and the group's official spokesman. He was killed in a car bomb explosion in 1972.[7] Although Kanafani was born into upper-middle-class urban society, the leveling experience of exile made him sensitive to the daily lives of more common folk. Many of his short stories and novels depict the individual's confrontation with occupation and exile, and in several of these the desert provides not only the physical setting but the antipode of the Palestinian sense of place.

The deserts in Kanafani's stories are real deserts. His 1957 short story, "Until We Return," opens with a Palestinian peasant making his way with difficulty across the soft sands of the Negev. The vicissitudes he encounters are physical, not existential—burning heat, relentless sun, thirst, and exhaustion. He is clearly a stranger in this place and ill equipped to cope with the environment's extremes. The peasant is headed for his former home to dynamite a water storage tank which the Israelis have built to irrigate lands he himself once tilled. The desert in this story is both a real environment, which many Palestinians crossed or attempted to cross after 1948 to return to their homes, and a test of the individual's will to resist. It is, however, secondary to the plot and Kanafani does not treat it in detail.[8]

Kanafani's use of the desert in his 1963 novel, *Men in the Sun*, is considerably more profound. Again it is a landscape of journey but one that leads to death rather than redemption. Three Palestinians, an older man with a family in a refugee camp, an unmarried young man with no means of getting ahead in life, and a teenage boy with a mother to support, are attempting to reach Kuwait, where each one dreams of making enough money to heal the pain and humiliation of homelessness. A Palestinian driver of a water tanker offers to smuggle them across the desert between Basra and Kuwait inside his empty water tank. The desert takes its toll when all three men suffocate to death in the heat of the tank while the driver, castrated in an explosion during the 1948 war, is held up by taunting border guards. After arriving in Kuwait, the driver is too exhausted to bury the corpses and instead abandons them in a garbage dump on the desert outskirts of the city.[9]

The burning desert in *Men in the Sun* is not simply the setting for the story nor a symbolic challenge, but a counterpoint to the land in which the characters once lived and a denial of their very existence. The characters' thoughts shift rapidly between present and past as the desert sun and glaring sands engulf their consciousness. At one point, the bright sun becomes the operating-room light under which the Palestinian driver had awaked to find himself castrated. At another point, the damp sand near the Shatt al-'Arab waterway in Iraq becomes the rain-moistened soil of the old man's lost field. As he turns to look up at the desert sky, thinking that the dirt must be wet from rain, he suddenly realizes where he is:

> [The sky] was burning white. A black bird circled high up, alone and directionless. He did not understand why but he was filled suddenly by a sickening awareness of homelessness. He felt he was on the verge of crying. Of course it hadn't rained yesterday. We're in August now, have you forgotten? The long road vanishing in the void like a black eternity, have you forgotten it? The bird still floated alone like a black dot in a vast white glare above him. We're in

August! Then why this moisture in the soil? It's the Shatt. Don't you see it stretching beside you there as far as the eye can see?[10]

Having momentarily regained consciousness, the old man's mind drifts forward and backward once again as he gazes at the oil-rich state of Kuwait across the water. His vision of it becomes a remembrance of his lost home. Although he clings to this mirage, he knows that reality will not live up to his expectations:

> Beyond the Shatt, just beyond it, lie all the things that are denied you. There lies Kuwait, the place that exists in your mind only as a dream and a fantasy. Surely it is something real, of stones and earth and water and sky, not like it floats in your overworked head. No doubt there are lanes and streets and men and women and children racing among the trees. No, no, there are no trees there. Sa'ad, your friend who went there to work as a driver and returned with bags of money, said there's not a single tree there. Trees exist only in your head, Abu Qays. In your old tired head, Abu Qays. Ten trees with twisted trunks that brought down olives and goodness every spring. There are no trees in Kuwait.[11]

The desert in *Men in the Sun*, tangible as it is, is not a fixed and well-defined place. It is a kind of "anti-place" which, while not defined, gives greater definition and coherence to the land left behind. The desert itself remains a blank, a landscape of indifference and death, and the journey through it is a journey to nowhere. Contemplating the sky, one character reflects on the fate of those who are strangers to the desert:

> The sun in the middle of the sky traced a wide dome of white flame over the desert while the trail of dust reflected a glare which nearly blinded the eyes. They used to say when someone didn't return from Kuwait that he had died, that sunstroke had killed him. He had plunged his shovel into the ground and then fallen over it. And so what? Sunstroke had killed him. Do you want him buried here or back there? That was all, sunstroke! And it's true! Who named it a stroke? Wasn't he a genius? As if this void was an unseen giant, lashing their heads with whips of fire and boiling pitch. But could

the sun really kill them and all this stench trapped within their chests?[12]

Kanafani's 1966 novel, *What Remains for You,* shows a further development of the desert as the antithesis of place. In this story, the desert becomes an actual sentient character. It feels the footsteps of Hamid, the young Palestinian boy from a Gaza refugee camp who sets out across the Negev to find his mother in Jordan. For Hamid the desert is not a counterpoint to the life he once led, for he is too young to have vivid memories of his original home in Jaffa. He only knows that when he lost Jaffa, he lost his mother, his self-respect, and everything else of value. He has grown up under the care of his spinster sister in Gaza, but when pregnancy forces her to marry a local man who is also a despised informer, Hamid feels humiliated. The situation impels him to leave in search of his mother and the security he has never had.[13]

Hamid's encounter with the desert occurs at night, so no burning heat or sun overwhelms his mind and memory. There is no escape to the brighter days of the past or dreams of the future as in *Men in the Sun.* Features and landmarks of the environment by which people could normally gauge their situation and orient themselves are hidden in the darkness. There is only the omnipresent desert, a palpable, uncompromising being which Hamid hates because it is too vast, yet must embrace because it is all that remains for him. At first frightened by its endless expanse, Hamid soon senses that it is not a threat, it is simply there:

> Suddenly his fear melted and vanished. No longer did anything exist except himself and this creature present with him, beneath him, inside him, breathing with an audible whistle, swimming majestically in a sea of gloom inlaid with stars.

He hears the motor of an Israeli jeep on night patrol:

> [The sound] appeared to him to be something totally expected. It would be impossible for anything in this vast expanse to be surprising. Nothing could be capable of being anything but small, clear and tame in this wide world exposed in all its power to everything.

As the jeep's searchlight sweeps the ground, Hamid presses himself against the desert sands:

> He felt [the desert] beneath him, shuddering like a virgin. As the beam of light brushed the folds of sand smoothly and silently, he pulled himself closer to the earth and felt it warm and soft. Suddenly the jeep appeared directly in front of him. He dug his fingers into the flesh of the ground and tasted its heat pouring into his body. It seemed to him as if it was breathing into his face, searing his cheeks.[14]

It would have been easy for Kanafani to portray the desert as sympathetic to the wandering Palestinian's plight, yet despite Hamid's intense feelings toward it, it remains essentially indifferent to his fate. It senses his footsteps, recognizes that he is going in the wrong direction, and wonders who this lone boy is, but harbors no empathy for him. It stirs no memories nor prods him toward a future goal. This is a landscape shorn of all meaning yet tangibly real, unlike the abstract images of the desert in the poems quoted earlier. In the course of his night journey, Hamid takes an Israeli soldier by surprise. Unable to proceed, but not knowing what to do with his captive, he simply sits and waits for whatever will happen next. The desert surrounds them, "violent, dry and unknown." He senses that both he and the Israeli

> feel together the expanse that never ends, the distance and strength and relentlessness surrounding them on every side, stretching farther than they could calculate and deeper than they could guess.[15]

This desert is pure space, lacking any feature of significance by which the protagonist might organize his experience and find his way. Kanafani never describes the particular environment of the desert in any of his works. His is not the desert of the nomadic Bedouin who knows every stone and mound, every place where an animal might hide, a plant grow, or a person find water. In fact, a character in *Men in the Sun* accuses the Bedouins of taking cruel advantage of Palestinians who lose their way in the desert.[16]

Kanafani recognizes the difference in the Bedouin's perception of the desert in "The Falcon," a short story he wrote in 1961 shortly after he left Kuwait. In this story a Palestinian engineer, working in the Gulf and living in a company compound isolated from the outside world "like an elegant cage," befriends a Bedouin watchman. The Bedouin tells a poignant story of his own homelessness away from the life of the desert he loves.[17] Although neither man comprehends the world from which the other came, they are equally trapped in a new reality which holds little meaning for them.

The desert is thus a real environment for many Palestinians in exile and a symbolic new landscape representing the transformation of place into space. This transformation involves the loss of boundaries, distinctive features, and internal structure which give character to place. The desert space contains no centers of meaning or framework or significance as did the Palestinian's own land, which itself had appeared ruined and empty to many nineteenth-century European eyes. The desert which Kanafani depicts is similar to the contemporary placeless landscape of the industrial West. Geographer Edward Relph describes this latter landscape as marked by confusion and proteanism "in which stability and consistency and the boundaries of things are not clearly defined." Increasing uniformity erases distinctive regional identities. Rational planning and mass technology create simple landscapes lacking subtlety or personality. A leveling of experience occurs in these landscapes in which an individual feels sensations but lacks any emotional involvement with his or her surroundings.[18]

The desert, despite being the antithesis of an urban industrial landscape, evokes for the Palestinian author a similar sense of placelessness. The boundaries and meanings Palestinians inscribed on their native land vanish in the desert of exile, leaving no context within which to make experience coherent. They cannot read the desert as the Bedouin does because they lack the experiences and the framework with which to connect themselves to that environment. Place becomes space, homogeneous and simple, yet overwhelming and alienating in its unbounded vastness. The desert has thus become a potent symbolic landscape representing the placelessness of exile in Palestinian literature.

THE CITY

Many Palestinian intellectuals took up residence in other Arab cities after 1948, specifically Beirut, Cairo, Damascus, and Amman, and in various European and American capitals. Younger refugees likewise found that the only alternative to life in a camp was life in a city. Thus the city is a frequent setting and symbol of Palestinian homelessness in the literature of older and younger writers alike.

When poets write of Palestine they usually name specific towns and villages. The city of exile, however, often remains anonymous, a technique that emphasizes the sense of detachment and placelessness. The setting of Tawfiq Sayyigh's "No. 24" is a typically nameless city:

> My feet are lacerated, homelessness has exhausted me,
> Park seats have left
> New ribs near my ribs.
> Policemen look askance at me,
> I drag myself from place to place,
> Destitute except for
> Day-long remembrances of a home
> That was mine yesterday—
> Only yesterday—
> And dreams
> In the evening
> Of my living in it again.[19]

The city of exile in Palestinian literature is unrelenting in its ugliness. It is associated with crowds, strangers, vermin, corrupt bureaucrats, and hucksters. In *Men in the Sun*, a fat Iraqi smuggler teases a Palestinian newcomer that he will be eaten alive by rats in his cheap hotel room. A Palestinian teenager in the same novel wanders through the crowded streets of Basra feeling utterly alone even among his Arab "brothers."[20] Tawfiq Sayyigh bitterly attacks the filth and aimlessness of the city, which refuses to provide him with comfort or meaning:

Extend O streets
And twist and darken
Emit your odors and aim the whispers well,
Hide ghosts in corners
Under half-lit lamps,
Cuddle your hags who natter in joy, in sorrow,
And wash yourself in gutters
That ever fill your potholes,
I do not come to you in the evening . . .
For fun to enjoy the sights
Taking, as it were, a dog for a walk
Or a delightful thought.
Your mud splattering my shoes and clothes,
Churning in my heart, my head,
Is my unpurging purgatory,
And my drifting in darkness
Is a repentant's counting
Of his beads for no salvation.
I walk your streets unwearied
Until, having said enough,
I add a few extra prayers
To end another night's expiation.[21]

That life in the city continues normally for others only alienates
the exile more. In his 1964 poem, "The Diary of the Epidemic
Year," Jabra Ibrahim Jabra expresses the anger of a stranger de-
nied a place:

On the sidewalk there are barefoot people laughing
The backgammon in the café is biased . . .
While my pocket is emptily screaming to God. . . .
In the crowd of those that shout
At death seeking the death of life,
There is no beauty anymore, no crimson lips, no large eyes. . . .
Let the voice of the muezzin rise in the ruins
Let the lute shed a dead tune
To a city whose walls and stones ooze of hatred,
But I was dreaming of green streets

And children running in them
And faces like laughing suns
Like lovers' faces wet with rain.
Here am I who did not cry except for the beautiful
Am weeping now for the lost roads
With no child running in them
Lips do not speak in them
Eyes are dark in them and hands
Are a blind chip of rock.
But on the sidewalk there are barefoot people laughing . . .
While my pocket is emptily screaming to God.[22]

Mahmud Darwish, who remained in Israel until 1971, wrote "Letter from Exile" before he himself left for exile. In the poem, a young man writes to his mother to assure her that he is doing well in the city, which is unnamed. He works in a restaurant, smokes on street corners, and flirts with girls like any other young man. Yet he fears darkness and hunger and is overwhelmed by the thought that if he should fall sick or die no one would know or care. Although he attempts to participate in the life of the city, the youth's activities are meaningless, serving only to mask his deep sense of alienation. Even his letter is an empty gesture, for no mail service operates between his place of exile and his mother's home in Israel.[23]

Rashid Husayn, another poet raised in Israel who left that country in the 1960s, attacked the luxury and corruption of the city of exile. Husayn, who was born into a peasant family in central Palestine, both participated in and despised the high life of a celebrated young exile artist. He died in a fire in his New York apartment at age forty, an alcoholic and alone. His poem, "At Zero Hour," depicts his feelings of hypocrisy and despair:

My God, rich and handsome, traveled aboard the most modern
    planes,
Kept my closest pals tucked away in banks,
And all the beautiful women he desired,
Geneva became his mistress,
Her bosom adorned with conference flowers.

My story is a little girl, born between Jaffa, Haifa and my love.
Nothing about her has changed;
I murdered the refugee camp a million times,
Yet nothing in it has changed;
I dwelled in hotels writing verses,
Nothing there has ever changed;
I saw the capitals of fifty diverse lands,
And nothing in me has changed.
I traced the outlines of my country upon my heart,
Turning myself into an atlas for her contours,
While she became the milk of my verse,
Yet nothing in it has changed.[24]

The exile city is much like the desert in its placelessness. The superficiality which Palestinian writers encounter there is akin to the barrenness of the desert. The city's alien character becomes more poignant by constant reminders that others feel at home. The landscape of the foreign city is a place for which the Palestinian has no responsibility and no sense of commitment. It is significant that, as in their depiction of the desert, Palestinian writers rarely describe the city of exile in detail. It lacks any particularity that would lend positive meaning and value to it. Like the desert, the city of exile represents the antithesis of a home place. Its lack of definition and substance serves to direct attention toward the home that once provided identity and value for the exiled writer. As a symbolic landscape of homelessness, it makes the focus on Palestine all the sharper.

THE REFUGEE CAMP

The refugee camp, the most squalid of all exile environments, is also the most ambivalent. It possesses all the elements of a symbolic landscape representing, like the desert and city, the placelessness of Palestinian experience: leaky tents, hastily built huts and tin shacks, long lines for food and medicine, poor sanitation, rain, cold, mud, and the endless wait for some news that will bring the nightmare to an end. Yet in some instances, the camp is also a potent symbol of resistance and steadfastness. Rashid Husayn's poem, "Tent #50 (Song of a Refugee)," encapsulates the harshness of the camp experience but ends on a characteristic note of defiance:

Tent #50, on the left, is my new world,
Shared with me by my memories;
Memories as verdant as the eyes of spring,
Memories like the eyes of a woman weeping,
And memories the color of milk and love!
Two doors has my tent, two doors like two wounds,
One leads to the other tents, wrinkle-browed
Like clouds no longer able to weep;
And the second—a rent in the ceiling—leading
To the skies,
Revealing the stars
Like refugees scattered,
And like them, naked.
Also the moon is trudging there
Downcast and weary as the UNRWA,
Yellow as though it was the UNRWA
Under a load of yellow cheese for the refugees.
Tent #50, on the left, that is my present,
But it is too cramped to contain a future.
And "Forget!" they say, but how can I?
    Teach the night to forget to bring
    Dreams showing me my village
    And teach the wind to forget to carry to me
    The aroma of apricots in my fields!
    And teach the sky, too, to forget to rain.
Only then may I forget my country.[25]

The camp in this poem is a landscape of despair and, like the desert and city, serves as a counterpoint to the refugee's memories of home. Its defiant ending, however, signals that it may also be a landscape of anticipation and hope entirely different from the desert and city. Fawaz Turki, a writer and poet who grew up in a

Beirut refugee camp, reflects on its dual personality in his memoirs:

> Man adapts. We adapted, the first few months, to life in a refugee camp. In the adaptation we were also reduced as men, as women, as children, as human beings. At times we dreamed. Reduced dreams. Distorted ambitions.

This is the camp of hunger, want, and hopelessness. But Turki goes on to describe listening to the old men as they sat and told stories, and he recalls an elderly poet reciting his verses late into the night:

> And we would know we were in a transplanted village that once was on the road to Jaffa, that once was to the north of Haifa, that once was close to Lydda.
>
> For if we had indeed acquired that "hate and bitterness" that the Western world claimed we were reputed for, we also danced the dabke, played the oud, and the women worked their embroidery. And those people outside the camp (not to mention those Western "tourists" with their blessed sympathy, their cameras, their sociology degrees, and their methodological and statistical charts), seeing our tattered rags hanging on us like white flags of surrender . . . did not know what we had. A feeling within us. Growing. A hope. The sad feeling of seeing a star, alone, at dawn. The waiting at a gap between the onrush of sounds.[26]

In the refugee camp, then, some sense of place is maintained by the presence of a community living together. This dual quality of camp life also dominates its portrayal in Ghassan Kanafani's works. "The Stolen Shirt" opens with a refugee father digging a ditch around his family's tent to prevent the mud and rain from sweeping it away. The rain is bitterly cold, yet he prefers to stay outside rather than face his hungry wife and son. His humiliation at being unable to provide for his family tempts him to join another Palestinian and a corrupt American UNRWA official in stealing flour from the camp's storehouse and selling it on the black market. While talking with the Palestinian, however, he is sickened by the thought of hungry refugees waiting for bread in tents all over his camp and in others like it. In a rage, he kills his companion, an act revealing that the refugee's spirit has not been completely extinguished. But the story ends on an ambivalent note. Returning to his tent, the father finds his son still hungry and ill clothed. The refugee has fought back but his homelessness has not been alleviated.[27]

Kanafani's novel, *Umm Sa'd*, offers a more complex image. Based on a real woman, according to Kanafani, Umm Sa'd is a middle-aged refugee mother living in a camp. The novel revolves around conversations between her and the narrator, an educated Palestinian. The camp is a wretched place, but its misery breeds strength in Umm Sa'd. In a long night of rain, her son mocks the camp's residents for their frantic efforts to avert flooding with shovels and pails. Umm Sa'd discovers later that he has left to join the fedayeen, the resistance fighters. To the surprise of the narrator, she rejoices in his departure despite her personal loss. The novel in general depicts the growing political consciousness of refugees and their rebellion against traditional Palestinian power structures, a resistance fueled by the camp's misery. The relation between Umm Sa'd and the narrator is perhaps most symbolic. Illiterate but resilient, Umm Sa'd has a grasp on the reality of her situation, but lacks the words to express herself. The narrator, educated but paralyzed by the camp experience, learns from her strength and at the same time gives voice to it.[28]

Despite its impermanence, poor housing, and insanitary conditions, the refugee camp has become a living symbol of struggle. It is not a homogeneous space, alien and meaningless like the desert and city. The Palestinians who live in the camps have shaped them into their own places. Mahmud Darwish relates the story of an Israeli soldier entering a camp after the 1967 war:

> He told me that when he entered one of the refugee camps he found that its residents were living exactly as they had lived in their former village. They were distributed just as they had been. The same village and the same streets. The soldier was irritated.
> "Why?"

"I couldn't understand. Nineteen years had passed and they still
said: 'We are from Bi'r al-Sab'!' "[29]

Re-creating certain aspects of home imbues the camp with
form and meaning otherwise absent in exile. Palestinian leadership
in maintaining and expanding camp schools, hospitals, businesses,
and social services likewise adds to a sense of responsibility and
commitment toward the camp as an important place. The fact that
many Palestinians opposed Israeli attempts to tear down ram-
shackle buildings in the Gaza Strip camps and replace them with
materially better, more permanent housing confirms the symbolic
status of the camp as a center of meaning and as a rejection of the
status quo.

The significance of the refugee camps was driven home for
Israelis and the rest of the world during the Intifada. On December 8, 1987, an Israeli-driven truck hit and killed four Palestinians,
among them residents of Jabaliya Camp in Gaza. There were immediate demonstrations and clashes with the army in Jabaliya, and
these quickly spread to other camps in Gaza and the West Bank,
marking the beginning of the Intifada, or uprising. Residents of
the camps were better organized to deal with curfews, blockades,
and other Israeli countermeasures than were their counterparts in
towns and villages where the uprising took a few weeks to get in
gear.[30]

EXILE AND THE DIALECTIC OF PLACE

How are these landscapes of exile significant? At an obvious level
they refute the idea, promulgated by the early Zionists and still
advanced in some Israeli circles, that the wide expanses of the Arab
world provide as good a home as any for Palestinians. In particular, many in the Israeli right have long argued that Jordan should
be the Palestinian homeland. In this scenario, the plight of exiles
is seen as purely territorial, a question of space.

The literary landscapes of exile, however, reveal the existential
nature of *al-ghurbah*. The deserts of the Arab world, while providing nearly limitless space, cannot provide a place, a home. To

the contrary, in their very boundlessness they make the loss of home and place all the more overwhelming and negating. Home is not just shelter, and place is not merely space. Exile towns and cities likewise negate the possibilities of home. One is always a stranger without power or standing, vulnerable to events beyond one's control. In both desert and city, Palestinians live at a disadvantage, lacking the experience and familiarity of natives. Life can take sudden nightmarish turns, as happened frequently in Lebanon and during the 1991 Gulf War and its aftermath when Arab governments expelled or fired Palestinian workers regardless of whether or not they had supported Iraq.

The depictions of the exile desert and city are not unique to Palestinian literature. They are archetypal expressions of what geographer Edward Relph calls "existential outsideness," a self-conscious uninvolvement with the world in which "all places assume the same meaningless identity and are distinguishable only by their superficial qualities." The result is alienation, homelessness, and a sense of the unreality of the world.[31] In this, Palestinian writing resembles other works of modern literature including the writings of European Zionists, who despaired of finding meaning and security in the Diaspora no matter how well assimilated they were.

The treatment of these landscapes is important to the Palestinian experience, however, because it starts to define one end of the new spectrum of Palestinian place and placelessness. It is in the dialectical nature of dwelling that place takes on highly explicit meaning when distinguished from its antithesis.[32] The definition of place includes what it is and what it is not, that is to say, some form of boundary is set.

The initial literary response to exile was to extol a dreamlike vision of a lost paradise while largely ignoring the contemporary fact of occupation and exile. By confronting *al-ghurbah* face to face, Palestinian authors in part overcame this nostalgic attitude and began to examine the more subtle qualities of their homeland brought out in the experience of homelessness. Fawaz Turki notes that this tension between environment and antienvironment has served to enrich the Palestinian sense of place, so that Palestine now suggests to a younger generation born in exile or under occupation "even more subtle, more enhanced nuances of meaning than it does to the generation that came before it."[33] Thus, while Palestinians may no longer be rooted in place, in the sense of being unself-consciously at home as they were prior to the advent of Zionism, they are developing a strong sense of place by self-consciously reconstructing a Palestine from which they gain a surer foundation in the world.[34]

This is more than a case of not appreciating what you have until it is lost. The articulation of a rhetoric of the land has historically played a critical role in supporting European and Zionist control over Palestine, much as it did in America and other colonial situations. Even Palestinians acknowledge that their land rhetoric has been much weaker than that of Zionists, putting them at a disadvantage in maintaining a communal sense of place in the face of exile and occupation, and especially in presenting their case to the outside world.[35] A peasant in Kanafani's story, "Until We Return," reflects that as the tiller of the land, he actually feels its substance and meaning, while others observe it merely as a passing view.[36] Other writers have also sought consolation from the belief that the Israelis will never know or love the land as intimately as the Palestinians.[37] The challenge, however, is to articulate this sense of place clearly and firmly so as to maintain it in new generations and to convey it to outsiders. Defining the landscapes of exile is one step in the process of articulation. The desert and city form the antipode of the Palestinian sense of place and mark its outer bounds. The refugee camp is an intermediate landscape in which a sense of place is delicately maintained and strengthened. It is now necessary to explore the new meanings and values Palestine itself is acquiring for Palestinians even as Israelis shape it into their own place.

CHAPTER 5

LANDSCAPES OF HOME

The ways in which Palestinian authors portray their homeland have evolved substantially since the establishment of Israel in 1948. As previously discussed, literature immediately following 1948 pictured a land of sweetness and fertility tinged by golden memories of childhood and youth. Essentially it was a nostalgic vision of a past place lost forever to the refugee. This image still exists in much exile literature and art. Fawaz Turki notes that it offers an emotional refuge in which the exile can establish a sense of at-homeness and security:

> And where else to do that but in a transplanted Palestine, a transplanted and reconstructed Palestine, a Garden where the Palestinian Adam, so familiar with his domain, finds nothing that he cannot name, nothing he cannot isolate, describe and explain.[1]

This mentally reconstructed Palestine is an aesthetic creation incorporating memories and ideals that can survive unperturbed in the individual's psyche. But it does not reflect contemporary experience and therefore tells us little of the Palestine that has been transformed by the state of Israel.

The Palestinians who remained in Israel after 1948, or who came under Israeli occupation in 1967, found themselves a minority among strangers who were rapidly reshaping the landscape. Nostalgic visions of the past were no longer tenable under such circumstances. A young woman in Emile Habiby's novel, *The Secret Life of Saeed, the Ill-Fated Pessoptimist*, argues with an old man who dreams of turning back time:

> Of his beginning an old man remembers only the prime of his youth and so thinks fondly of it. Do you really know how the beginning was, uncle? The beginning was not merely sweet memories of pines over Mount Carmel, or orange groves, or the songs of Jaffa's sailors. And did they really sing anyway?[2]

To the younger generation of Palestinians growing up in Israel, nostalgic images were an impediment to creating and maintaining a sense of enduring identity. Mahmud Darwish, born in the village of Barwah near Acre in 1942, was a key figure in resistance literature inside Israel until he left the country in 1971. In the early 1960s, he was already criticizing the hollow aestheticism and rhetorical abstraction of traditional poetry. Its simple symbolism and nostalgic themes, he argued, had become bankrupt in the face of Israel's growing dominance. Attacking a popular analogy between Palestine and the lost Arab golden age of Muslim Spain, Darwish wrote that the idea of a lost paradise "seduces poets who lack anything else to move them, [but] brings to the Palestinian situation only a flood of tears and tired blood."[3] In a 1964 poem he bitterly criticized traditional motifs that no longer spoke to the current context of political and social upheaval:

> Yesterday we sang for stars above clouds
> And were sunk in tears!
> Yesterday we rebuked the vine trellis, the moon,
> The night and fate,
> And tried to flatter women!
> The hour struck and Khayyam was getting drunk,
> On the narcotic beat of his songs
> We remained wretched. . . .
> Our poems are without color
> Without taste . . . without sound!
> If they don't carry the lamp from house to house,
> If simple souls don't understand their meaning,

Then it's better to cast them off
And stay silent.
If only these poems were
A chisel in the grip of a worker,
A grenade in the palm of a fighter!
If only they were!
If only these words were
A plow in the hands of a peasant,
A shirt or a door or a key!
If only they were![4]

Darwish's call for poets to speak the language of the common folk and to write about daily life and work was representative of a new generation of Palestinian poets and novelists in Israel. Many of these writers came from lower- and middle-class families in villages and small towns. Educated in Israeli-supervised schools, they grew up isolated from mainstream Arab literary movements. Most are fluent in Hebrew and well acquainted with Israeli society; indeed, some found an early forum for their work through the support of Rakah, the Israeli Communist party. It is in the work of these poets and authors that we find attempts to articulate a Palestinian sense of place within Israel and the occupied territories.

LITERARY PALESTINE—IMAGES OF PLACE

In contrast with stark portrayals of exile, literary evocations of Palestine convey dense detail. While monotony, homogeneity, and hostility characterize exile, poets and novelists fill the landscape of Palestine with the familiar everyday features of home. This tendency also contrasts with pre-1948 works in which the homeland was often abstract and monolithic, an ideological construction designed to advance nationalist aims. Beginning in the 1950s and especially in the 1960s and later, Palestinian poetry and prose shifted to focus on rural land and life. Authors reconstructed features of the folk landscape, trying to recapture in words and images a natural, spontaneous relationship between Palestinians and their environment. Such an intense focus on the rural landscape was a new departure for Palestinian literature. Urban intellectuals previously knew little about nor cared for life in the countryside. The hero in Habiby's novel, *The Secret Life of Saeed*, besieged by displaced villagers wanting news of their homes, remarks in confusion that "we of Haifa used to know more about the villages of Scotland than we did about those of Galilee."[5] Now, however, the link with the land in a literal rather than an abstract sense of homeland has become a fundamental motif through which Palestinian authors define their identity and present their case to the world.

The use of landscape to refer to literary depictions of the environment can be misleading in Palestinian writing. Unlike the earlier portrayals by Western visitors or Zionist visionaries, there are few sweeping vistas of mountain, plain, valley, or town. Rather it is the foreground, to continue the pictorial analogy, which fills the Palestinian literary landscape. The focus is on material elements in the immediate environment, and the horizon rarely extends beyond nearby fields.

Several writers describe this foreground in minute detail, as if reconstructing in words every inch of space. Anton Shammas's 1986 novel, *Arabesques*, is unrelenting in its thick description of home. In one passage, the main character recalls how dynamite explosions from a nearby quarry regularly shook his windows and "the glazing of the kerosene lantern suspended from the iron bar hanging down from the keystone of the arch that supported the ceiling of our house."[6] In another passage he reconstructs the family's cistern:

> The cupboard where we kept our mattresses and blankets, the *smandra*, which was the color of green olives, stood hugging the western wall of our house. It concealed the door behind which, in the thick wall, was an archway that led outside. Set in the threshold of that archway was the mouth of the cistern. A grayish metal lid with a ring in its center covered the mouth, and this protected the cool water in the darkness of the cistern from the whims of children and cats and from falling leaves, which during the days of summer

had made the circles of light that seeped through their profuse foliage dance on the sides of the archway.[7]

Shammas's insistence on rendering every detail of home contrasts with his more superficial description of milieu when his characters move outside their home territory. In these situations detail is given to the characters and their actions more than to place. Yet the thick description of home is in the end an enigma when we discover that the characters are not who we think they are, and that the details which they have described may or may not be real.

In poetry, the insistence on detail is more straightforward but also manifests a fear of being swept into unreality. The various parts of the house—its stone walls, mud roofs, hearth, door, and courtyard—carry intensely emotional meanings. Poets employ them as symbols of identity, security, and resistance. Darwish's desire that words become "a shirt or a door or a key" reflects this persistent emphasis on the material minutiae of everyday life. Articulation of these details is a way to grasp and limit reality, to hold on to something concrete and close at hand in a world that is otherwise slipping away. Tawfiq Zayyad's poem, "A Letter across Mandelbaum Gate," sends greetings to a refugee mother from her house, fireplace, pots, and pans.[8] Darwish asks his mother in a poem to use him as fuel for her oven or as a clothesline on their roof. Without this link to her daily life, his own life feels aimless and without purpose.[9] Mu'in Bisisu likens a man who resisted the authorities to "the solid wall of a house in Gaza."[10]

From the house and courtyard, the landscape expands to the village fields and pastures. It is still an insider's view—there is little scenery in the sense of wide vistas. Rather, individual commonplace features become invested with heightened meaning. The trees and crops that once formed the economic base of Arab Palestine appear frequently. In particular, the olive tree, which, as noted earlier, held substantial practical, emotional, and spiritual value for the residents of pre-Zionist Palestine, has evolved into a symbol of communal rootedness, identity, and resistance. Critic Raja' al-Naqqash notes that the symbolic use of the olive tree is appropriate to the Palestinian struggle. Needing only a small space to grow and able to survive on limited rainfall, the olive tree is both well adapted to the natural environment and a reliable source of support for peasant farmers. The peasant's personal attachment to the tree and its deep and long-living roots in the soil symbolize a steadfast bond between Palestinians and the land.[11]

In Anton Shammas's *Arabesques*, a torn and abandoned sack of olives embodies the depth of the 1948 disaster. An Arab comes to loot the home of a Palestinian resistance leader who had earlier humiliated him but who has now fled from approaching Jewish forces in the midst of the 1948 war. Looking around the house for goods to collect, the intruder spies "a frayed sack of olives standing in the corner of the kitchen. Trailing out of its bulging belly were green olives, which had spilled onto the kitchen floor, their thin glistening skin seeming to be on the point of exploding from the pressure of the oil held within." The looter breaks down sobbing at this sight, which signifies a household suddenly abandoned in the midst of daily life, its precious commodities left behind. "The frayed sack of olives made tangible what he himself could expect within just a few hours, for his fate and the fate of [his adversary] were the same."[12]

In Tawfiq Zayyad's "On the Trunk of an Olive Tree," the tree forms a final bulwark against the progressive transformation of the land:

> Because I do not weave wool
> And every day I'm in danger of being arrested
> And my house open to police visits
> To search and to "clean,"
> Because I am unable to buy paper,
> I shall carve all that has happened,
> All my secrets,
> On an olive tree
> In the courtyard of the house.
> I shall carve my story and all the seasons of my tragedy,
> My sighs,
> My grove and the tombs of my dead.
> I shall carve the number of every usurped plot
> Of our land,
> The location of our village and its boundaries,

Its people's houses that have been razed,
My uprooted trees,
And every wildflower that has been crushed. . . .
I shall carve "Kafr Qasim,* I will not forget,"
I shall carve "Dayr Yasin,* it has taken root in my memory" . . .
I shall carve all that the sun tells me,
What the moon whispers to me,
And what the lark relates
At the well forsaken by its lovers.
In order to remember
I shall remain here carving . . .
On the olive tree in the courtyard of the house![13]

The poet invests the olive tree with his memories, experiences, and hopes. Like the house, the use of the olive is a means of giving concrete form to an intangible sense of place that is under threat. Other features that stand out in the poetic articulation of place include wheat, vineyards, orange groves, and fig, almond, and mulberry trees. Even stones, inert and seemingly neutral, become repositories of value because they belong to the land and are integral parts of the human environment. The unarticulated role such features once played in folk perceptions has evolved. Commonplace features now carry explicit symbolic meaning and help to define the landscape of home.

Just as writers depict the commonplace in the material environment, so their portrayal of events occurring in this setting focuses on the activities of everyday life rather than on unusual happenings or heroic adventures. Emile Habibi's short story, "The Junk Dealer," tells of an aging Arab woman in Israel who collects things left behind by refugees who fled in 1948. She patiently preserves old letters, photographs, and other mementos of daily life

*Kafr Qasim was the site where Israeli frontier police in 1956 killed 49 peasants returning home from work. They had not been informed that a curfew had gone into effect that afternoon. Dayr Yasin was the village where commandos of the Zionist underground organization Irgun massacred 250 Arab villagers in 1948 in an effort to spread panic among Arabs so that they would flee their homes.

in the expectation and hope that their owners will one day return.[14]

The Druze poet Samih al-Qasim uses images of daily life to concretize the loss of home in immediate, visceral terms:

> I speak to the world of a ewe not milked,
> Of a morning coffee not drunk,
> Of a mother's dough not baked,
> Of a mud roof gone to weed,
> I speak to the world . . . I tell it![15]

The exceptional simplicity of al-Qasim's imagery creates a powerful and effective poem. By contrasting lived experience before and after the disruptions caused by the emergence of Israel, the poet is able to capture the poignancy of the individual's loss. At the same time, he gives expression to the bonds with place created in carrying out the activities of daily life, bonds which normally remain unconscious and unarticulated. Literature's emphasis on the routines of everyday life becomes a means for preserving an intimate knowledge of local environments, whose character the Israelis aim to refashion into their own places.

NATURE AS ADVOCATE AND ARGUMENT

The use of place imagery in literature helps Palestinians, as individuals and as a group, to maintain a sense of belonging to a particular place and milieu. But it also sends a message to the outside world by incorporating nature and the local environment into the political argument. Poets and novelists depict the microworld of rural life, for example, to emphasize the Palestinian's close link to nature and the land. This link is, in turn, a fundamental buttress of their argument for self-determination. The stress on the personal and material aspects of the bond between people and land rather than on its aesthetic values gives added strength to their cause. Darwish's poem, "On Steadfastness," makes this point explicit:

We love the rose
But we love wheat more.
We love the essence of the rose
But the spike of grain is purer,
So protect your grain from these times
With your chest, immovable from its place,
Let us make a wall of chests,
Of chests, then how could it be broken?
Grasp the spikes of grain
As you would grip a dagger!
The land, the peasant, persistence,
Tell me how can these be subdued?
This trinity, how can it be overcome?[16]

This poem reflects Darwish's involvement with Communism and Palestinian nationalism. Rural land and life have long provided symbols of communal solidarity in Western nationalist literature. Darwish's literary skills allow him to effectively draw upon environmental imagery for political purposes. As critic Hanan Ashrawi points out, however, there is a tendency in much of Palestinian literature for the symbolism to become "frozen," each symbol automatically representing some standard meaning rather than the imagery suggesting a larger, united whole. Ashrawi argues that many poets "string together the familiar series of images and symbols to come up with a nationalistic poem. These poems remain fragmentary without any internal unity and development, relying mostly on the emotional appeal of the topic itself."[17] Thus olives, almonds, figs, wheat, and corn represent the goodness of the land, jasmine and lilies express its beauty, and the sun, sky, and stones signify the people's steadfastness and yearning for freedom. Storms, thunder, and lightning stand on occasion for the forces of evil and at other times for the cleansing violence of rebellion.

Israeli censorship is also partly responsible for the development of this conventional symbolism. Susan Slyomovics, in an essay on Palestinian theater during the Intifada, observes that Israeli censorship is much stricter with artistic works of theater, literature, painting, and music than with journalistic reportage. The Israeli government's practices in this regard reflect the power of these creative efforts.[18] Environmental features are, on the surface, politically neutral, yet they are well understood to represent something else. The olive tree is a convenient means of signifying Palestine without using the actual word. A hope for the coming of "eastern winds" refers to the expectation of Soviet and Arab socialist aid. 'Asifah, the word for storm, is also the name of a Palestinian commando group; Darwish's famous poem, "Promises from the Storm," is a salute to these fighters, who could not otherwise be identified.

Ashrawi views frozen symbolism as a major flaw in Palestinian literature. Yet even the mediocre use of environmental imagery reveals the deeper significance given to nature in contemporary literature, a significance that was not dominant before 1948. A shift toward a greater awareness of nature, particularly the land, is a frequent response to disruption and displacement. Franz Fanon, generalizing from the Algerian revolution, argues that "for a colonized people the most essential value . . . is first and foremost the land; the land which will bring them bread and dignity."[19] James Turner, in a study of English topographic poetry during the turmoil of the seventeenth century, notes that "when reality is permeated by violence, 'nature' is asked to oppose, criticize and, if possible, replace it."[20]

This is clearly true in contemporary Palestinian literature. Authors enlist nature in general, and the land in particular, as their last and strongest ally. Whereas the Israelis establish their place by transforming nature—draining swamps, irrigating arid lands, and building cities, Palestinian writers cling to the indigenous landscape and its relict features for inspiration and support. This supportive, defensive role assigned to the surrounding home environment contrasts sharply with the indifference and hostility of exile. The use of pathetic fallacy portrays nature as sympathetic to the poet's mood and situation. Two poems by Mahmud Darwish exemplify this idea. The first, "Three Pictures," depicts the moon, like the poet, as cold, sad, and lost:

> The moon was
> As it had been since we were born, cold.

The sadness in its face poured out
In streams . . . streams flowing
Towards the enclosure round the village.
It sank sadly,
A fugitive.[21]

In "A New Address," on the other hand, nature imparts to the poet a childlike sense of pleasure:

Even the moon was dear to this place,
It seemed more beautiful and larger,
The scent of the land was like a perfume
And the taste of nature sweet,
As if I was on the roof of my old house
With a new-born star taking up its place right before my eyes.[22]

In Jabra Ibrahim Jabra's novel, *The Search for Walid Mas'ud*, rain provides an evocative metaphor for the thoughts and feelings of the title character, a native of Bethlehem, as he walks through the streets of his hometown:

Rain. How sweet it is, how bitter. Love, fear, anticipation; all these things I feel for the rain. I watch for it, I want it to continue and to stop at the same time. The sound of rain drumming, pounding, wheezing, excites me. It makes me want to sing and love. It makes me want to fade away and die. The rain used to come down so hard it filled the valleys and the roads and made a mockery of our flimsy houses. It leaked through the roof exposing the innermost secrets of the houses. . . . Everything seems bleak, old or decrepit, still the rain pours down. Rain, rain . . . with the rain life can burst forth, black change into green, the old begin to dance and the dead bloom once more. I wept silently while my face was buffeted by the wind and rain. I mourned my dead brother, my murdered people, my friends and my nation. . . . The rain kept pounding on the doors and windows, trying to penetrate the houses, to uncover the depths of human secrets, to flow into hidden nooks and crannies, presaging death and saving from death those whom I love . . . the rain proclaiming life to glow, to rage, to love, to reproduce life.[23]

The encounter with rain expresses the character's ambivalent feelings toward the world in which he lives. The rain is depressing, like the city's streets and houses, and reminds him of the tragedies he has experienced. Yet it is also a balm like tears, softening the harshness of the present. The rhythmic patter of rain conveys a sense of unity with the cyclical nature of life. The resurgence of life after winter rains offers hope that his life, too, will be renewed despite current tribulations. Although Jabra lives in exile, writers in Israel employ similar rain imagery to express the soft sadness of nature in sympathy with the Palestinian.

Anton Shammas's depiction of a cistern, quoted earlier, similarly asserts a bond with the natural world. His character in *Arabesques* recollects the sound of winter rainwater falling into the deep cistern at night:

> When my ear lay close upon the pillow, I could hear the spattering of the water, swathed in echoes, falling down the shaft to the bottom of the cistern. The spatters grew fainter and fainter and shed their echoes as the water level rose in the cistern, until nothing was heard but moans of repletion, rising and surfacing from the throat of the cistern, for the water pouring down threatened to make the swelling cistern overflow. That was the time when the drainpipe was turned away from the shaft to spill its torrent down the winding path to our fig grove at Al-Jahaleef.[24]

These images contrast sharply with the highly critical treatment given to Israeli irrigation projects. They are regarded as unnatural, mechanized intrusions which aid and abet Israel's usurpation of the land. Rain belongs to the old, natural landscape where its coming was a blessed event heralding new life and hope. In literature, rain—natural, life-giving, unsusceptible to Israel's domination—becomes a symbol of nature's alliance with the Palestinian.[25]

The importance of nature goes beyond support and inspiration.

In many poems and novels, land and person merge, reflecting the author's yearning to be at one with the land and partake of its strength and resistance. The land is seen as a product of its inhabitants' lives and labors. The peasant and the land are part of each other's essence. In Darwish's portrayal of his deceased grandfather, the old man is barely distinguishable from the earth in which he is buried:

> Face of my grandfather! Cheerless prophet!
> What grave sends you forth,
> Wearing a vest the color of rock, stained with ancient blood,
> Garbed in a cloak the color of soil? . . .
> Sorrow of a field that holds mortal remains,
> Olive trees and tired winds.[26]

In other cases, the poet becomes the land personified, thirsting for redemption. A poem by Rashid Husayn expresses this desire to be the earth itself. Husayn beseeches a cloud to rain on him, for he is all that remains of the usurped land:

> I am the land . . . do not deny me rain,
> I am all that remains of it.
> Plant my brow with trees
> And turn my poetry into vineyards
> And wheat
> And roses
> That you may know me,
> And let the rain pour down.
> I, cloud of my life, am the hills of Galilee,
> I am the bosom of Haifa,
> The forehead of Jaffa. . . .
> Can you not see the veins of my brow
> Striving to kiss your lips?
> Waiting for you, my poetry turned to earth,
> Became fields,
> Turned into wheat
> and trees.
> I am all that remains of our earth,

I am all that remains of what you love,
So pour . . . pour with bounty,
Pour down the rain.[27]

The desire to physically unite with the land is intensified by metaphors of sexual love. Darwish's "A Lover from Palestine," perhaps his best-known work, exemplifies this need, but other examples abound. 'Abd al-Latif 'Aql, a West Bank poet, declares to his lover, Palestine:

In times of drought you are my figs and olives,
Your barrenness is my fragrant gown.
Of the rubble that was your eyes I erect my home,
I love you alive, I love you in death.
When hungry I feed on thyme.
I feel your hair against my face and I pine,
My weary face turns red.
I am born in the palms of your hands, an embryo,
I grow and grow, I reach maturity.
I drink the meaning of life from your gaze,
Then my being is awakened and intoxicated. . . .
When I am led all alone
To be whipped and humiliated,
And lashed at every police station,
I feel we're lovers who died from ecstasy,
A dark-skinned woman and a dark-skinned man.
You become me and I become you—
Luscious figs and shelled almonds.[28]

A physical union between author and land is the culmination of the attempt to express through symbols an entrenched relation between Palestinians and their homeland, a relation that can be maintained and reinforced in the face of Israeli rhetoric invoking the land. What was once an unarticulated attachment to the local milieu of house, village, and field has now been coded in symbols and images.

Yet the creation of this symbolic landscape and its accompanying rhetoric is problematic. At an obvious level, metaphors of sexual union between male authors and the female land are not likely to resonate with Palestinian women. Here it is helpful to recall Layla 'Allush's poem, "The Path of Affection," quoted in Chapter 1. In this poem, 'Allush unites land with people, but through the metaphor of family. On a journey to meet relatives in Haifa, the narrator notes all the changes the Israelis have wrought, yet the earth itself remains unchanged and resolutely Arab. In it she sees her own Arab countenance mirrored, as we recognize the features of our face in a close relation. Like a family member, the land also recognizes the narrator:

> O my grandparents, the rich soil was bright with Arab reserve,
> And it sang out, believe me, with affection.[29]

This last line evokes the image of an Arab homecoming celebration with its ululations, embraces, food, and laughter. The difference between the two metaphors—familial and sexual—involves expressions of power. The family's persistence and strength derive from intimate, familiar bonds of affection and love, developed and tested through long experience together. The family works as a metaphor for the land by invoking this intimate bond, which is unattainable for newcomers no matter how much they manipulate surface appearances. The sexual metaphor works more explicitly by representing a more aggressive battle for possession. Through its use the (male) author asserts his ownership of the land over his Israeli rival. But this possession, while more declarative and strongly worded, is also more vulnerable and desperate. It is the act of an individual apart from community, and it acknowledges the presence of a powerful rival who may take away possession. The land as female is the object of a wrestling match, and in its objectification it becomes in some sense up for grabs.

The problematic nature of consciously constructing a land rhetoric, or sense of place in Yi-Fu Tuan's terms, reveals itself in the dynamics of this wrestling match. Zionists came to Palestine with a land rhetoric already at hand, and sought to replace its overworked words with the unarticulated, unquestioned bonds that grow from experience. In attempting to do this, they have in many ways forced Palestinian writers to move in the opposite direction—to create a persuasive and encompassing rhetoric as a replacement for experience over which they have lost control. If place, home, and territory are defined in part by their antitheses, then these must be explored. In confronting these antitheses, Palestinian authors have had to reflect on the dialectics of place existing between themselves and Israelis, a painful process which opens both new wounds and new possibilities.

CHAPTER 6

ENCOUNTERING ISRAEL

Ⅰn the problematic nature of people and place, the articulation of the relationship between the two is both necessary and destructive. It is necessary in that words can be translated into power and action, but destructive in that so much that is meaningful is inexpressible in the common parlance of power and is thus marginalized. In the act of creating a powerful language of place, we begin to speak and think in symbolic and often simplistic terms which distort essential meanings and experiences. Mahmud Darwish writes about how Israeli claims to home changed his own understanding:

> They didn't just occupy the land and its activities alone; they occupied the inner mind and temperament and the bond between you and your home, so that you begin to question the very meaning of this home.[1]

Raja Shehadeh, in his book, *The Third Way,* also reflects on this dilemma, which he first recognized in a conversation with American Jewish author Robert Stone. In referring to the land, Stone had made an analogy with pornography:

> When you are exiled from your land, he said, you begin, like a pornographer, to think about it in symbols. You articulate your love

for your land, in its absence, and in the process you transform it into something else.

"We Jews had 2,000 years in which to become expert pornographers with a highly symbol-wrought, intellectualized yearning for this land—totally devoid of any memories or images of what it really looked like. And when Jews came to settle here this century, they saw the land through these symbols. Think of the almost mystical power that names of places here have for many Zionists," Robert said. "As for what it really looked like, they tried to transform it into the kinds of landscapes they left in Europe."

Later Shehadeh examined his own feelings about the land and discovered that he, too, was becoming a "pornographer":

Sometimes, when I am walking in the hills . . . unselfconsciously enjoying the touch of the hard land under my feet, the smell of thyme and the hills and trees around me, I find myself looking at an olive tree, and as I am looking at it, it transforms itself before my eyes into a symbol . . . of our struggle, of our loss. And at that very moment I am robbed of the tree; instead there is a hollow space into which anger and pain flow.[2]

Shehadeh realizes that a land rhetoric is necessary for maintaining self-identity and for opposing Israel's efforts to deny Palestinians a place. Yet he is angered when the rhetoric robs him of the land's material essence. The Israelis are not only physically reshaping Palestine into Israel, they are forcing the Palestinian to reshape his or her emotional and spiritual attachments to the land. The land necessarily becomes part of the political argument. Its trees, houses, fields, and hills are no longer unquestioned elements of the places where Palestinians dwell; they must do battle with the places that the Israelis are constructing. The olive tree, as a naive focus of experience, is forever lost, as is the rest of the local landscape. This personal loss profoundly affects Shehadeh:

I feel deep, deep resentment against this invasion of my innermost imagery and consciousness by the Israelis. As a child I took for granted a natural pleasure in this land . . . but since the occupation,

I have begun to think of our hills as "virginal," "molested" by the Israeli bulldozers—the bulldozers that have become for me the symbol of Israeli power over us. I am sure that my imagery would not be so replete with sexual-political symbols were I left to the privacy of my feelings. I can thank our occupiers, then, among other things, for instilling in me a political pornographer's eye for this land.[3]

Clearly, the ways in which writers and poets create a Palestinian landscape reflect Israel's claims and activities. Certain aspects of nature and features of the environment acquire highly political value as writers use them to combat the adversary's rhetoric. Other features may go unnoticed because they do not form part of the national symbolic landscape. The landscape of Israel is the antithesis of Palestine, and as Darwish and Shehadeh both observe, it plays a significant role in sensitizing and shaping Palestinian perceptions.

THE LANDSCAPE OF ISRAEL

Israel in the eyes of Palestinian writers is a simplified environment. What Israel has erased is as important as what it has built. Writers refer to villages that no longer exist and Arab houses now occupied by Israelis. In contrast to earlier nostalgic laments over lost homes, however, more perceptive authors recognize and wrestle with the meaning of Israel's transformation of the land. Ghassan Kanafani, in *Return to Haifa*, presents an emotional encounter between an Arab couple from the West Bank, who are allowed to visit their former home in Haifa after the 1967 war, and an elderly Jewish refugee from Nazi Europe, who has built a safe and secure life in what was the couple's house. She and her husband also adopted and raised the infant boy found in the house, who was mistakenly left during the panic of battle in 1948. Kanafani acknowledges the transformation that has taken place. The house is no longer defined by its being the lost home of an Arab family. The Jewish woman has made it her own by living in it and caring for it. After hearing that their lost son is alive, the parents are

shocked to meet him, a young and proud Israeli soldier who cas-
tigates them for never even trying to find him. The novel is a
scathing critique of the nostalgia and self-pity prevailing among
upper-class Palestinians who refused to confront the reality of Israel after 1948.[4]

The struggle over names of towns, streets, and natural features
is another part of the transformation of Palestine into Israel. In
some instances, as discussed in Chapter 1, the Israelis gave biblical
names to Arab towns and villages identified as historic Jewish sites.
In other cases, new Hebrew names were coined. Darwish recounts
a taxi trip during which the Moroccan Jewish driver, not realizing
that his passenger is an Arab, condemns the continued use of any
Arab street names. Arriving at his destination, al-Mutanabbi Street
(al-Mutanabbi was a famous tenth-century Arab poet), Darwish
himself wonders why its Arab name has been spared. Looking
more closely at the Hebrew street sign, he discovers that it reads
"Almont Navi," a Hebraicized transformation of the Arabic and
an obliteration of its cultural meaning.[5]

Only a few writers treat in detail what the Israelis have added
to the landscape. Some perceive Israel as a Western imitation,
blatantly maladapted to the true Palestinian environment. Israel
is simple, homogenized, mechanized, and prefabricated, imposed
on the land rather than harmonizing with it. Layla 'Allush notes
"the hybrid signs, shops and cemeteries," "the seas of light and
technology," and the "fresh fertilizers and efficient sprinklers"
which have come to dominate the Israeli landscape.[6] Israelis take
enormous pride in these accomplishments and use them as a jus-
tification for their possession of the land. That Palestinians did not
create similar "miracles" when the land was theirs constitutes in
Israeli eyes a forfeiture of ownership. Palestinians, on the other
hand, view this Israeli "miracle" with deep suspicion and hostility.
Mechanized irrigation on Jewish land has caused many springs
and wells on Arab land to dry up.[7] Urban and suburban expansion
have swallowed up Arab villages and lands. New buildings in sub-
urbs and in Jewish settlements whose residents commute to work
in the city are, as Palestinians picture them, faceless white blocks
strangely devoid of life. Their bright reflective whiteness by day
and well-lighted aspect at night contrast with the more muted

tones of traditional Arab towns and villages. Raja Shehadeh describes a visit to 'Isawiyyah, a village engulfed by the Israeli expansion around East Jerusalem:

> I had never been to 'Isawiyyah before. I drove through the concrete jungle Israel has built on Mount Scopus in East Jerusalem—the new Hebrew University buildings and the densely built residential towers of the French Hill. I knew 'Isawiyyah was hidden somewhere below, and I stopped someone and asked him how to get there. He gave me detailed instructions but still I lost my way. Every time I thought I was on the road out, it somehow turned back on itself, leading deeper into the maze. I was closed in by columns of windowless, towering monsters, covered in glaring white, machine-sawed stone facing.
>
> I don't know how, but suddenly I found I was on a road leading out towards a village, into another world, with terraced housing merging softly with the round hills they hugged . . . a scattering of tiny man-made homes tucked away below the Israeli fortresses.[8]

Shehadeh also remarks on the prefabricated houses used in Jewish settlements on the West Bank, houses which symbolize the incongruity of the Israeli presence on the land. The sight of a house built elsewhere and dropped from a truck onto the ground seems strange and threatening to Arab eyes:

> The traffic was stopped while a big carrier truck carrying a whole, ready-made, pre-fabricated house with windows, a bathroom, a living room, a kitchen, pipes—a home—was negotiating a difficult bend. . . . Then came another and a third and a fourth—six in all. . . . Near our car, a woman with her child was standing. "See the houses of the Jews," she said. Her son wanted to stay and watch but she snatched him away and continued walking.[9]

Apart from large agricultural projects and settlements, Palestinian writers regard Israel correctly as a predominantly urban society. This sharply contrasts with the old village landscape of Palestine as envisioned by Palestinians and, ironically, with Israeli images of themselves which still play up the pioneering perspective of a heroic rural landscape peopled by farmer-soldiers. In Palestinian literature, urban images of worker exploitation, big money, high living, and dubious entertainment come to the fore. In Sahar Khalifah's novel, *'Abbad al-Shams* (Sunflower), a traditional and somewhat naive widow from Nablus becomes embroiled with an Arab prostitute when she ventures into Tel Aviv to sell the shirts she has sewn.[10] Another of Khalifah's novels, *Subar* (published in English as *Wild Thorns*), portrays the experiences of West Bank men working as low-paid, unskilled laborers in Tel Aviv with few rights or benefits. One of the main characters, the son of a once-prosperous Nablus family, fears revealing that he has joined this daily dawn exodus of laborers, insisting to his sick father that he is still tending their family's lands, which in fact have been economically strangled by the migration of workers to Israel. Local merchants, unable to match the low prices of food and other goods from Israel flooding the local market, likewise find their lives and businesses devastated.[11]

Samih al-Qasim laments the transformation of traditional elements of the Palestinian landscape into urban amusements for newcomers and visitors:

> So what,
> When the almond and the olive trees have become timber
> To adorn tavern doorways,
> And to be made into statues
> Whose nudity beautifies parlors and bars
> And are carried by tourists
> To the ends of the earth
> While nothing remains before my eyes
> But dry leaves and tinder.[12]

Palestinian writers clearly perceive and react against Israeli attempts to expropriate the land's history as solely their own and to market that history at home and abroad. Recall Darwish's encounter with the young Jewish shepherd from Yemen who believed that the rubble of Darwish's village came from an ancient Roman town.[13] The notion of a previously forsaken landscape rediscovered has now been packaged for consumption. Shehadeh recounts overhearing an Israeli tour guide describing olive trees as having descended from those planted by Abraham. In another instance he stopped to listen as an Israeli tour guide led tourists through Jaffa:

> I saw through his listeners' eyes the "cute" Israeli "reconstructions" of Old Jaffa; the site of my romantic longings plastered over into art galleries, discos, expensive restaurants, fancy shops. No tourist or Israeli my age could ever guess that thirty-five years ago this was the vibrant, flourishing Arab centre of Palestine. No trace of it is left; its people are scattered all over the world.[14]

Archaeology, the key component in the Israeli presentation of history both to themselves and the outside world, takes on a sinister and conspiratorial hue for similar reasons. Palestinians regard it as an attempt to establish Israel's roots while at the same time denying the link between Palestinians and their homeland. Darwish expresses the bitterness and defiance felt by Palestinians in confronting Israeli historical claims:

> The archaeologist is busy analyzing stones,
> Searching for his eyes in the rubble of legends
> In order to certify
> That I am merely a passer-by on the road,
> Without eyes or words in the scripture of civilization!
> But I go on slowly planting my trees,
> Singing about my love![15]

THE STRUGGLE OF ENCOUNTER

"Without eyes or words in the scripture of civilization" recalls Moshe Shamir's description of the shepherd who watched as young boys from the kibbutz engaged in mock battle.[16] The shepherd uttered sounds understandable only to his flock, sounds which mesmerized Shamir but which were devoid of civilized meaning for him and the other kibbutzniks, and thus devoid of challenge or threat. The shepherd is the kind of Arab that Shamir, an award-winning writer, former leftist, and later cofounder of the far-right Tehiya (Renaissance) Party,[17] respects and with whom he feels comfortable. Confusion and unease begin, Shamir writes, when Israelis meet educated, urban Arabs, "a confusion you never sensed when in the company of the 'ordinary Arab.' "[18] This confusion arises, Shamir argues, when Israelis attempt to treat these educated Arabs, who look and talk like Israelis, as the equals of Israelis. In *My Life with Ishmael*, Shamir puts an end to this confusion by launching into thirty-five pages of instructions for ways "the educated Arab" can confront and surmount the basic deficiencies of Arab culture. These include corruption, deceitfulness, and an utter lack of "social backbone" and "any independent national quality."[19] At the end of this learning process, Arabs will attain rational faculties and recognize that peace and coexistence are the solutions for their predicament.

Shamir even provides the educated Arab's reply to his instructions, putting it into the mouth of a "young, handsome, pleasant-mannered, self-confident Arab poet with the impertinent charm . . . of a rising star, who used to frequent Bohemian circles in Tel Aviv."[20] Shamir claims to know this reply by heart and so dispenses with any need to listen. Thus even the educated Arab who lives by words is rendered mute and powerless. It is Shamir's contention that the Arabs must recognize their powerlessness before they will be able to advance their society.[21]

Shamir in effect answers the confusion existing between Israelis and Palestinians by demanding that Arabs be silent until they learn to speak in a parlance acceptable and comprehensible to Israelis. Significantly, the figure of the mute Arab plays a pivotal role in the work of another respected Israeli writer, A. B. Yehoshua. In Yehoshua's story, "Facing the Forests," however, the silence of the Arab is disturbing and intensifies confusion.[22]

The protagonist of "Facing the Forests" is a rootless, brooding Israeli student writing a thesis on the Crusades. He exemplifies the dilemma felt by many Israeli Jews born and raised in the state of Israel who remain plagued by questions about their place in the land and the world at large. Far from being self-confident natives full of hope and idealism, they are alienated, frustrated urbanites who can never live up to the expectations and exploits of their pioneering parents. The Israeli student in the story is urged by friends to work as a fire-watcher in one of Israel's forest reserves. These forests, like other nature reserves, are often used as a method of land seizure, and ceremonial tree planting and the sponsoring of forest sites is something of a national obsession.[23]

In the story, as in some real instances, the forest reserve has been planted over the ruins of an Arab village. The reserve is also the home of a mute Arab whose tongue has been cut out. The fire-watcher reluctantly begins to familiarize himself with the forest and with the Arab, who he fears will try and burn the forest down. As he comes to know the woods more intimately, the fire-watcher becomes obsessed with the Arab village he never knew existed. After halfheartedly trying to burn the forest himself, to the fascination of the Arab, the fire-watcher lectures the Arab on the Crusades. The Arab listens and later starts making "confused, hurried gestures, squirming his tongue, tossing his head. He wishes to say that this is his house and that there used to be a village here as well and that they have simply hidden it all, buried it in the big forest."[24]

In the end, with the fire-watcher's complicit acceptance and encouragement, the Arab burns the forest, revealing the ruins. In this conspiracy of destruction, the Israeli loses all his possessions, including the notes for his thesis, but gains a sense of history and possession by participating in an act of transformation, albeit one which destroys what his parents have built. For his part, however, the mute Arab remains powerless and homeless, despite his act of rebellion.

For all its intense symbolism, Yehoshua's story remains ambiguous, and it has inspired conflicting interpretations among Israeli commentators. Some see it as anti-Zionist and some as the birth of a new Zionism which speaks to the post-pioneer generation of native-born Israelis.[25] But whatever the conclusion, the story depicts the construction of a place through the destruction of another place, a struggle between memories.

This struggle continues to evolve and change shape. Mahmud Darwish reads Yehoshua's story as acknowledgment that Israel has built itself on the ruins of Arab homes, and as an admission of wrongdoing (which may in fact be reading too much into the tale). Yet this admission, he argues, comes more easily when one is in a position of unchallenged power.[26] Like the mute Arab, Darwish and others still struggle with the words to relate their story and to wrestle with the story of their adversaries.

Anton Shammas, an Arab Christian Israeli, wrote that he once pictured himself as Yehoshua's mute Arab facing the forests.[27] His novel, *Arabesques,* in many ways epitomizes the confusion and struggle between Jew and Arab in Israel. As noted earlier, the novel is dense with the detail of daily Palestinian life, and yet Shammas wrote it in Hebrew. The author explained in an interview that "you cannot write about the people whom you love in a language that they understand; you can't write freely."[28] The narrator, also named Anton Shammas, relates much of the detail based on his family lore, but like a recurring dream, the details change from telling to telling. Also like a dream, missing pieces of the family puzzle prevent it from forming a coherent whole. Interwoven with the family story is another tale of the narrator as writer encountering an Israeli Jewish novelist who is determined to create the perfect Arab character. The effect of *Arabesques* is to put all aspects of identity in question and to challenge both memory and intent. Above all, the book wrestles with words and their ability to both illuminate and obfuscate.

THE QUEST FOR HOME

The literary rendering of Palestine creates an intensely felt dilemma at the same time as it provides a genius loci for Palestinian identity. The creation of a highly articulate and conscious symbolic landscape necessitates a process of abstraction, much like the drafting of a map. Real places are not found on maps, only their abstraction in the form of lines, points, and labels. While drawing the boundaries of nations or property is a primary means of possession, this act of abstraction also makes the lines vulnerable to argument, negotiation, assault, and dispossession. Boundaries become objects open to manipulation.

The articulation of home likewise necessitates its abstraction and objectification. To even engage in debate about what home means becomes an acknowledgment that one is no longer at home. This paradox lies at the core of Darwish's essay, "Home . . . Between Memory and a Suitcase," an anguished analysis of one seemingly simple question: what is home? It's not a map, Darwish writes, nor a birth certificate. It's not where you were born, nor where you will die. It's not the land of your ancestors because the adversary claims the same. These easy answers might have sufficed before Israel was established, but now they all ring hollow. Darwish continues: "It's not a question that you can answer and continue on your way. It's your life and your cause bound up together. And before and after all of that, it's the essence of who you are."[29]

Darwish addresses his essay in the second person to a Palestinian reader who appears to be Darwish himself, and in this voice he describes how the meaning of home evolved in his life. He tells of the child who fled to Lebanon in the dark of night during the 1948 war when his village came under attack from Jewish forces:

> If it were not for the moon that night, they would have lost you forever . . . as a mother from Haifa did on a moonless night. Her house under assault from bullets and explosions, she grabbed what she thought was her child and jumped into the nearest boat. At sea after leaving port she discovered that her "child" was only a pillow, and from that day since she has been mad. How many children changed to pillows and pillows to children? And what is home? The home of a mother is her child, and the home of a child is its mother.[30]

In Lebanon as a refugee, Darwish continues, "you know for the first time what home is. It's the thing that is lost, the awaited return." But upon that return Darwish finds that he is the one who is lost. Like the mute Arab, he cannot utter the word *Palestine,* nor admit to having been in Lebanon for fear of being labeled an infiltrator. Instead his family assures authorities that he was with Bedouin nomads in the northern part of the country. The village of al-Barwah, meanwhile, had been razed to the ground and Yemeni Jews given the surrounding fields to till. Darwish writes, "The moment they arrived on your land, they defined the parameters of their existence and those of their children. And at the same time they defined yours. The moment they became natives you became a refugee."[31] The second meaning of home for the refugee thus becomes longing for both the land and one's rightful claim, not the land alone but the right as well: "Whereas their claim originated in tears and memories, it now became land and power. You, without power, lost history, land and claim."[32]

It is from this realization that Darwish proceeds to analyze the meaning of home not as a one-sided longing for place, but as a struggle between two memories: "The Israeli refuses to coexist with the Palestinian memory, refuses to recognize it. Despite the fact that one of their national slogans is 'We shall never forget.' " Darwish recognizes that remembrance of the Holocaust is a means of solidifying national consciousness, in that Israel is the only guarantee of security for Jews. He admonishes Palestinians to remember Nazi butchery as well and never succumb to the anti-Jewish hatred of the Nazis. "No matter to what degree the hostility between Israeli and Arab may rise," he writes, "no Arab has the right to feel that the enemy of his enemy is his friend, for Nazism is the enemy of all peoples."[33]

In an Israeli artists' colony Darwish meets a man who fled from the Nazis. The colony in which he lives is called Ein Hod, which was formerly an Arab village called 'Ayn Hawd. Israeli artists have preserved the stone houses as a testament to the aesthetic of folk architecture, while the original Arab residents have constructed new houses on a hill overlooking the site.[34] The Israeli artist tells Darwish that the Arab decor reminds him of the East. Darwish questions how he can feel at home if he needs Arab decor to provide a sense of home. The artist-cum-refugee replies, "I have no other option."[35] Recognizing that they are both refugees, and that the affirmation of one results in the negation of the other, Darwish concludes that home is a struggle, an ongoing process. "Between memory and a suitcase, there is no other solution but struggle."[36]

Palestinian writers have established a symbolic landscape of meaning and value as a way of defining their place in the world. The house, courtyard, village, trees, and other features prominent in the Palestine of memories figure just as prominently in the contemporary geography of Palestinian literature. In and among these features stands the writer, seeking, like the Zionist of an earlier period, boundaries and security. And yet it seems that neither can find the rootedness they seek. "Your need to demonstrate the history of stones," Darwish tells Israelis, "does not give you prior membership over him who knows the time of the rain from the smell of the stone."[37] Palestinian writers attempt to maintain this essential meaning of stones as a means of confronting and resisting Israeli versions of place, history, and identity. In the process, however, stones necessarily become an intellectual effort for Palestinians as well. These efforts grant rhetorical power but at the same time expose the vulnerability of words, for when words fail in confrontation with power, stones become weapons.

NOTES

CHAPTER 1

1. Mahmud Darwish, *Yawmiyat al-Huzn al-'Adi*, p. 64.
2. Ibid., p. 40.
3. Raja Shehadeh, *The Third Way*, pp. 86–89.
4. Darwish, *Yawmiyat al-huzn al-'adi*, p. 61.
5. See the discussion of place in Edward Relph, *Place and Placelessness*, especially pp. 29–43.
6. Christopher Alexander, Sara Ishikawa, and Murray Silverstein, *A Pattern Language*.
7. Anne Buttimer, "Home, Reach, and the Sense of Place," in *The Human Experience of Space and Place*, ed. Anne Buttimer and David Seamon.
8. Kevin Lynch, *The Image of the City*.
9. Jay Appleton, *The Experience of Landscape*.
10. Relph, *Place and Placelessness*, p. 40.
11. Ibid. See also Yi-Fu Tuan's books, *Topophilia* and *Space and Place*; David Seamon's *A Geography of the Lifeworld*; David Lowenthal and Martyn Bowden's edited collection, *Geographies of the Mind*; and Donald Meinig's edited volume *The Interpretation of Ordinary Landscapes*.
12. Yi-Fu Tuan, "Rootedness versus Sense of Place," *Landscape* 25 (1980): 3–8.
13. Martin Heidegger, "Building, Dwelling, Thinking," in his *Poetry, Language, and Thought*. See also Christian Norberg-Schulz's interpretation of Heidegger's thought in *Genius Loci: Towards a Phenomenology of Architecture*.

14. Kimberley Dovey, "Dwelling, Archetype and Ideology: Unpacking the Dwelling Experience," keynote address presented at The Dwelling Symposium, The University of Texas at Austin, School of Architecture, April 1992.

15. Maurice Natanson, *Literature, Philosophy and the Social Sciences*, pp. 96–97; see also Yi-Fu Tuan, "Literature, Experience, and Environmental Knowledge," in *Environmental Knowing: Theories, Research, and Methods*, ed. Reginald G. Golledge and Gary T. Moore.

16. *HaOlam Hazeh*, June 15, 1983 (reprinted in *Al-Fajr*, July 1, 1983, p. 7).

17. Layla 'Allush, "The Path of Affection," in *The Palestinian Wedding*, trans. Abdelwahab M. Elmessiri, pp. 173–175.

CHAPTER 2

1. Yehoshua Ben-Arieh, *The Rediscovery of the Holy Land in the Nineteenth Century*, p. 15.

2. W. J. Stracey, "Palestine as It Is and as It Might Be," *Palestine Exploration Fund Quarterly Statement* (October 1880): 241–242.

3. Ibid.

4. William M. Thomson, *The Land and the Book*, pp. 347–348.

5. Meron Benvenisti, *Conflicts and Contradictions*, pp. 195–196.

6. Ben-Arieh, *The Rediscovery of the Holy Land in the Nineteenth Century*, p. 232.

7. Ibid., p. 12.

8. Thomson, *The Land and the Book*.

9. G. Robinson Lees, *Village Life in Palestine*, preface.

10. Ibid., p. 1.

11. See the discussion in Sarah Graham-Brown, *Palestinians and their Society: 1880–1946*.

12. Thomson, *The Land and the Book*, p. xvi.

13. Graham-Brown, *Palestinians and their Society*, p. 42.

14. Jacob M. Landau, *Abdul-Hamid's Palestine*, pp. 10, 15.

15. James Turner, *The Politics of Landscape*, pp. 194–195.

16. Ben Halpern, "Zion in Modern Literature: Hebrew Prose," in *Zion in Jewish Literature*, ed. Simon Halkin, p. 121.

17. Hillel Bavli, "Zion in Modern Literature: Hebrew Poetry," in *Zion in Jewish Literature*, ed. Halkin, p. 102.

18. Walter Laquer, *A History of Zionism*, pp. 75–79; Gila Ramras-Rauch, *The Arab in Israeli Literature*, pp. 9–11.

19. Laquer, *History of Zionism*, pp. 84–135.

20. Halpern, "Hebrew Prose," p. 133.

21. See the discussion concerning Arab-Jewish relations in Laquer, *A*

History of Zionism, pp. 209–269; see also the chapters by Chaim Weizmann, David de Sola Pool, and Ephraim Broido in *The Jewish National Home: The Second November*, ed. Paul Goodman (London: J. M. Dent, 1943).

22. Laquer, *History of Zionism*, pp. 168–169, 277–294; Ramras-Rauch, *The Arab in Israeli Literature*, pp. 8–12; Alan R. Taylor, "Vision and Intent in Zionist Thought," in *The Transformation of Palestine*, ed. Ibrahim Abu-Lughod, pp. 14–15.

23. Quoted in Laquer, *A History of Zionism*, p. 61.

24. Quoted in Bavli, "Hebrew Poetry," p. 104.

25. Laquer, *History of Zionism*, pp. 220–221, 277–278; Ramras-Rauch, *The Arab in Israeli Literature*, pp. 11, 37–38; Yosef Gorny, *Zionism and the Arabs 1882–1948: A Study of Ideology*, pp. 66–72, 130–132; Simha Flapan, *Zionism and the Palestinians*, pp. 199–208.

26. John Ruedy, "The Dynamics of Land Alienation," in *The Transformation of Palestine*, ed. Abu-Lughod, p. 130.

27. Gorny, *Zionism and the Arabs*, pp. 26–27.

28. Ibid., pp. 42–45; Ramras-Rauch, *The Arab in Israeli Literature*, pp. 4–6.

29. Gorny, *Zionism and the Arabs*, pp. 45–51, 61–67; Ramras-Rauch, *The Arab in Israeli Literature*, pp. 4–6.

30. Ramras-Rauch, *The Arab in Israeli Literature*. Evolving perspectives on Arab as both native son and enemy in Israeli writing is a central theme throughout Ramras-Rauch's very illuminating study. She includes a brief chapter on the Canaanite movement (pp. 113–117). For the philosophy of Nissim Malul, see Gorny, *Zionism and the Arabs*, p. 48.

31. Bavli, "Hebrew Poetry," p. 111.

32. Laquer, *A History of Zionism*, p. 209.

33. Interview in the *Sunday Times*, June 15, 1969.

34. Salma Khadra Jayyusi, *Trends and Movements in Modern Arabic Poetry*, vol. 1, pp. 270–271.

35. Alexander Schölch, "European Penetration and the Economic Development of Palestine, 1856–82," in *Studies in the Economic and Social History of Palestine in the Nineteenth and Twentieth Centuries*, ed. Roger Owen, pp. 39–54; Landau, *Abdul-Hamid's Palestine*, pp. 35–95.

36. Graham-Brown, *Palestinians and their Society*, p. 35.

37. Ruedy, "Land Alienation," pp. 122–124; Schölch, "European Penetration," p. 56; Joel S. Migdal, *Palestine Society and Politics*, pp. 12–14.

38. Schölch, "European Penetration"; Hannah Margalit, "Some Aspects of the Cultural Landscape of Palestine in the First Half of the Nineteenth Century," *Israel Exploration Journal* 13 (1963): 216–217.

39. Tawfiq Canaan, "Plant-Lore in Palestinian Superstition," *Journal of the Palestine Oriental Society* 8 (1928): 138–140.

40. Graham-Brown, *Palestinians and their Society*, pp. 40, 54, 113; Tawfiq Canaan, "The Palestinian Arab House," *Journal of the Palestine Oriental Society* 13 (1933): 64.

41. Canaan, "The Palestinian Arab House," p. 55.

42. Ibid., pp. 61–63.

43. Ibid., p. 68.

44. Ibid., pp. 70–72.

45. Tawfiq Canaan, "Modern Palestinian Beliefs and Practices Relating to God," *Journal of the Palestine Oriental Society* 14 (1934): 79.

46. Tawfiq Canaan, "Mohammedan Saints and Sanctuaries in Palestine," *Journal of the Palestine Oriental Society* 4 (1923): 1–84.

47. Canaan, "Modern Palestinian Beliefs," pp. 83–85.

48. Ibid., pp. 85–86.

CHAPTER 3

1. Quoted in Walter Laquer, *A History of Zionism*, p. 198.

2. Simon Halkin, *Modern Hebrew Literature*, pp. 90–91.

3. Laquer, *History of Zionism*, pp. 295–308.

4. Ibid., p. 320.

5. For a discussion of the development of this image and its consequences for Israeli policies, see S. Waterman, "Ideology and Events in Israeli Human Landscapes," *Geography* 64 (1979): 171–181.

6. Halkin, *Modern Hebrew Literature*, pp. 121–122.

7. Ibid., p. 201.

8. Ibid., p. 200.

9. Ibid., pp. 176–177.

10. Ibid., pp. 128, 188.

11. Ibid., pp. 205–206.

12. Ibid., p. 114.

13. Meron Benvenisti, *Conflicts and Contradictions*, pp. 19–23.

14. Waterman, "Ideology and Events," p. 172.

15. Moshe Shamir, *My Life with Ishmael*, p. 154.

16. Ibid., p. 153.

17. Benvenisti, *Conflicts and Contradictions*, pp. 193–194.

18. Ishmael, in Hebrew, or Isma'il, in Arabic, was the son of Abraham by Hagar and in Islam is considered to be the originator of the Arab branch of the Semite people.

19. Shamir, *My Life with Ishmael*, p. 154.

20. Salma Khadra Jayyusi, *Trends and Movements in Modern Arabic Poetry*, vol. 2, pp. 367, 532.

21. Ibid., pp. 675–678.

22. Poem by Elias Marmura, quoted in 'Abd al-Rahman Yaghi, *Hayat al-Adab al-Filastini al-hadith*, pp. 127–128.

23. M. Peled, "Annals of Doom: Palestinian Literature 1917–1948," *Arabica: Revue d'études arabes* 29 (1982): 153–156.

24. Translation by Salma Khadra Jayyusi, in Jayyusi, *Trends and Movements*, vol. 1, p. 287.

25. Ibrahim Tuqan, *Diwan Ibrahim*, pp. 69–70.

26. Quoted in M. Peled, "Annals of Doom," pp. 177–178.

27. Al-Aqsa Mosque, the third most holy site in Islam, occupies the Haram al-Sharif, the area from which Muhammad ascended to Heaven during his miraculous night journey to Jerusalem. Al-Buraq is the name of the horse which Muhammad rode on this journey. It is, in addition, the traditional name given by Jerusalem's Muslims to the western section of the wall enclosing this area, also known as the Western Wall or Wailing Wall (see Wadi' al-Bustani, *Diwan al-Filastiniyat*, p. 194). The Dome of the Rock is a larger mosque adjacent to al-Aqsa. Both these mosques stand on the Temple Mount, the ancient site of the First and Second Temples of the Hebrews. The Church of the Holy Sepulchre marks the traditional site of Jesus Christ's crucifixion and burial.

28. See, for example, Tuqan's "al-Quds," in *Diwan Ibrahim*, p. 67.

29. Quoted in Jayyusi, *Trends and Movements*, vol. 1, p. 296.

30. Quoted in Peled, "Annals of Doom," p. 179.

31. See, for example, the following references in al-Bustani's *Diwan al-Filastiniyat*, pp. 120, 186–187, 193–194.

32. See, for example, Tuqan's poem, "Hittin," in *Diwan Ibrahim*, pp. 50–54; and the discussion by Peled, "Annals of Doom," pp. 167–168.

33. See, for example, the poem by al-Abushi, quoted in 'Abd al-Rahman al-Kayyali, *al-Shi'r al-Filastini fi nakbat Filastin*, p. 119; and the poem by Hasan al-Buhayri quoted in Peled, "Annals of Doom," p. 181; also the discussion in Yaghi, *Hayat al-adab*, p. 304.

34. For a discussion of the roles of poetry and prose in this period, see Peled, "Annals of Doom," pp. 151–163.

35. Ibid., pp. 157–158.

36. Ibid., p. 154.

37. Yaghi, *Hayat al-adab*, pp. 512–513.

38. See Peled, "Annals of Doom," pp. 160–162.

39. Quoted in Yaghi, *Hayat al-adab*, pp. 500–501.

40. Quoted in Yaghi, *Hayat al-adab*, p. 514.

41. Janet Abu-Lughod, in a demographic study of population changes in Palestine, estimated that the events of 1948 displaced between 770,000 and 780,000 Palestinians. See her article, "The Demographic Transformation of Palestine," in *The Transformation of Palestine*, ed. Ibrahim Abu-Lughod, pp. 139–164, especially p. 161.

42. Ghassan Kanafani, "Adab al-muqawama ba'da al-karithah," in his *al-Athar al-kamilah*, vol. 2, p. 38.

43. Jabra Ibrahim Jabra, "The Rebels, the Committed and the Others: Transitions in Arabic Poetry Today," *Middle East Forum* 43 (1967): 21.

44. Translated in Mounah Khouri and Hamid Algar, eds., *An Anthology of Modern Arabic Poetry*, pp. 225–226.

45. "Nada' al-ard," in Fadwa Tuqan, *Diwan Fadwa Tuqan*, pp. 153–161.

46. "Dari" [My House] in Harun Hashim Rashid, *Diwan Harun Hashim Rashid*, p. 261. Abu Salma, a fiery nationalist poet prior to 1948, also wrote a sentimental poem about his house after his exile.

47. 'Abd al-Karim al-Ashtar, *Dirasat fi adab al-nakbah: al-riwayah*, pp. 13–23.

48. Quoted in A. L. Tibawi, "Visions of the Return: The Palestinian Arab Refugee in Arabic Poetry and Art," *Middle East Journal* 17 (1963): 511.

49. "Ma'a al-ghuraba'," in Rashid, *Diwan Harun Hashim Rashid*, pp. 7–13.

50. Quoted in Tibawi, "Visions of the Return," p. 514.

51. Raja Shehadeh, *The Third Way: A Journal of Life in the West Bank*, p. 88.

52. Quoted in Tibawi, "Visions of the Return," p. 515.

53. Quoted in Tibawi, "Visions of the Return," p. 513.

CHAPTER 4

1. Estimates of the numbers of displaced persons vary widely due to the inadequacies of census data and to political sensitivities on all sides. The figures used here come from Jane Abu-Lughod's "The Demographic Transformation of Palestine," in *The Transformation of Palestine*, ed. Ibrahim Abu-Lughod, pp. 153–163; and from Peter Beaumont, Gerald H. Blake, and J. Malcolm Wagstaff, *The Middle East: A Geographical Study*, p. 387.

2. Beaumont et al., *The Middle East*, pp. 405–410.

3. Quoted in A. L. Tibawi, "Visions of the Return: The Palestinian Arab Refugee in Arabic Poetry and Art," *Middle East Journal* 17 (1963): 521.

4. Translated in Mounah Khouri and Hamid Algar, eds., *An Anthology of Modern Arabic Poetry*, pp. 225–229.

5. From the poem, "On One Single Face," in *The Palestinian Wedding*," trans. Abdelwahab M. Elmessiri, pp. 137–141.

6. From Fadwa Tuqan, *Diwan Fadwa Tuqan*, p. 522.

7. Hilary Kilpatrick, "Tradition and Innovation in the Fiction of Ghassan Kanafani," *Journal of Arabic Literature* 7 (1976): 53–54.

8. "Ila ʿan naʿud," in Ghassan Kanafani, *Al-Athar al-kamilah*, vol. 2, pp. 791–801.

9. "Rijal fi al-shams," in Kanafani, *al-Athar al-kamilah*, vol. 1, pp. 29–152.

10. Ibid., p. 38.

11. Ibid., p. 46.

12. Ibid., pp. 131–132.

13. "Ma tabaqqa lakum," in Kanafani, *al-Athar al-kamilah*, vol. 1, pp. 153–233.

14. Ibid., pp. 168–169.

15. Ibid., p. 218.

16. "Rijal fi al-shams," in Kanafani, *al-Athar al-kamilah*, vol. 1, p. 112.

17. "al-Saqr," in Kanafani, *al-Athar al-kamilah*, vol. 2, pp. 423–436.

18. Edward Relph, *Place and Placelessness*, pp. 133–137.

19. Quoted in Issa J. Boullata, "The Beleaguered Unicorn: A Study of Tawfiq Sayyigh," *Journal of Arabic Literature* 4 (1973): 78.

20. "Rijal fi al-shams," in Kanafani, *al-Athar al-kamilah*, vol. 1, pp. 67, 73.

21. Quoted in Jabra Ibrahim Jabra, "The Rebels, the Committed and the Others: Transitions in Arabic Poetry Today," *Middle East Forum* 43 (1967): 26–27.

22. In Issa J. Boullata, trans. and ed., *Modern Arab Poets: 1950–1975*, pp. 109–111.

23. "Risala min al-manfi," in Mahmud Darwish, *Diwan Mahmud Darwish*, vol. 1, pp. 56–68.

24. Translated in Elmessiri, *The Palestinian Wedding*, pp. 179–181.

25. Translated in Naseer Aruri and Edmund Ghareeb, eds., *Enemy of the Sun*, p. 11.

26. Fawaz Turki, *The Disinherited: Journal of a Palestinian Exile*, pp. 45–46.

27. "al-Qamis al-masruq," in Kanafani, *al-Athar al-kamilah*, vol. 2, pp. 781–790.

28. "Umm Saʿd," in Kanafani, *al-Athar al-kamilah*, vol. 1, pp. 235–335. See also the discussion of the novel in Muhammad Siddiq's *Man Is a Cause: Political Consciousness and the Fiction of Ghassan Kanafani*, pp. 62–71. Hilary Kilpatrick has translated an extract of Umm Saʿd in her collection of Kanafani stories—see Ghassan Kanafani, *Men in the Sun and other Palestinian Stories*, pp. 77–79.

29. Mahmud Darwish, *Yawmiyat al-huzn al-ʿadi*, p. 57.

30. Adil Yahya, "The Role of the Refugee Camps," in *Intifada*, ed. Jamal R. Nassar and Roger Heacock, pp. 91–106.

31. Relph, *Place and Placelessness*, p. 51.

32. Ibid., p. 49.

33. Fawaz Turki, "Meaning in Palestinian History: Text and Context," *Arab Studies Quarterly* 3 (1981): 375.

34. See the discussion by Yi-Fu Tuan in "Rootedness versus Sense of Place," *Landscape* 25 (1980): 3–8.

35. See, for example, Raja Shehadeh, *The Third Way: A Journal of Life in the West Bank*, pp. 84–89.

36. "Ila 'an na'ud," in Kanafani, *Al-Athar al-kamilah*, vol. 2, p. 795.

37. Shehadeh, *The Third Way*, p. 89.

CHAPTER 5

1. Fawaz Turki, "Meaning in Palestinian History: Text and Context," *Arab Studies Quarterly* 3 (1981): 376; see also his article, "Alienation of the Palestinian in the Arab World," in *Settler Regimes in Africa and the Arab World*, ed. Baha Abu-Laban and Ibrahim Abu-Lughod, pp. 119–124.

2. Emile Habiby, *The Secret Life of Saeed, the Ill-Fated Pessoptimist*, trans. Salma Khadra Jayyusi and Trevor Le Gassick, p. 154.

3. Mahmud Darwish, *Yawmiyat al-huzn al-'adi*, pp. 33–34.

4. "'An al-shi'r," in Mahmud Darwish, *Diwan Mahmud Darwish*, vol. 1, pp. 91–95.

5. Habiby, *Secret Life*, p. 22.

6. Anton Shammas, *Arabesques*, trans. Vivian Eden, p. 37.

7. Ibid., p. 47.

8. "Risalah 'abr bab mandalbawm," in Tawfiq Zayyad, *Ashaddu 'ala aydaykum*, pp. 102–105.

9. "Ila ummi," in Darwish, *Diwan Mahmud Darwish*, vol. 1, p. 162.

10. Mu'in Bisisu, "No," in *The Palestinian Wedding*, trans. Abdelwahab M. Elmessiri, p. 155.

11. Raja' al-Naqqash, *Mahmud Darwish: sha'ir al-ard al-muhtallah*, pp. 186–188.

12. Shammas, *Arabesques*, p. 119.

13. "'Ala jidh'i zaytunah," in Tawfiq Zayyad, *Umm Durman*, pp. 29–35.

14. "Umm al-rababikiya," in Emile Habibi, *Sudasiyat al-ayyam al-sittah*, pp. 29–35.

15. "Ahki lil-'alam," in Samih al-Qasim, *Dukhkhan al-barakin*, pp. 38–39.

16. "'An al-sumud," in Darwish, *Diwan Mahmud Darwish*, vol. 1, pp. 69–72.

17. Hanan Mikhail Ashrawi, "The Contemporary Palestinian Poetry of Occupation," *Journal of Palestine Studies* 7 (1978): 90–92.

18. Susan Slyomovics, " 'To Put One's Finger in the Bleeding Wound': Palestinian Theatre under Israeli Censorship," *The Drama Review* 35 (1991): 27–28. Slyomovics points out that Israeli censors are even more strict with films and theatrical performances than with published literature because of the potentially more dangerous communal response to the enactment of political art, as opposed to the individual act of reading.

19. Quoted in Naseer Aruri and Edmund Ghareeb, eds., *Enemy of the Sun*, p. xxxvi.

20. James Turner, *The Politics of Landscape*, p. 7.

21. Quoted in al-Naqqash, *Mahmud Darwish*, pp. 178–179.

22. Ibid.

23. From Jabra Ibrahim Jabra, *al-Bahth ʿan Walid Masʿud*, pp. 241–243 (passage trans. by Elizabeth Fernea and Lena Jayyusi in *Modern Arabian Short Stories*, ed. Salma Khadra Jayyusi).

24. Shammas, *Arabesques*, pp. 47–48.

25. For references to rain in poetry, see the following poems in Elmessiri's *The Palestinian Wedding*: Rashid Husayn's "To a Cloud" (p. 103) and Walid Halis's "Mayy and Other Primitive Things" (pp. 129–135). See also Mahmud Darwish's poems in *Diwan Mahmud Darwish:* "Wa ʿada . . . fi kafan" (vol. 1, pp. 29–40), "Matar" (vol. 1, pp. 185–189), "Matar naʿim fi kharif baʿid" (vol. 1, pp. 406–410), and "al-Matar al-awwal" (vol. 1, pp. 471–474). For references to Israeli irrigation see Layla ʾAllush's "The Path of Affection," in Elmessiri's *The Palestinian Wedding* (pp. 173–175) and Ghassan Kanafani's "Ila an naʿud" in his *al-Athar al-kamilah* (vol. 2, pp. 791–801).

26. "To my Grandfather," in Elmessiri, *The Palestinian Wedding*, p. 145.

27. "To a Cloud," in Elmessiri, *The Palestinian Wedding*, p. 103.

28. "Love Palestinian Style," in Elmessiri, *The Palestinian Wedding*, pp. 117–119.

29. Layla ʾAllush, "The Path of Affection," in Elmessiri, *The Palestinian Wedding*, pp. 173–175.

CHAPTER 6

1. Mahmud Darwish, *Yawmiyat al-huzn al-ʿadi*, p. 69.

2. Raja Shehadeh, *The Third Way: A Journal of Life in the West Bank*, pp. 86–89.

3. Ibid.

4. "A'id ila Hayfa," in Ghassan Kanafani, *al-Athar al-kamilah*, vol. 1, pp. 337–414.

5. Darwish, *Yawmiyat*, pp. 90–91.

6. Layla 'Allush, "The Path of Affection," in Elmessiri, *The Palestinian Wedding*, trans. Abdelwahab M. Elmessiri, pp. 173–175.

7. See, for example, Sahar Khalifah, *'Abbad al-shams*, and Samih al-Qasim's "Watan," in his collection, *Dammi 'ala kaffi*, pp. 62–64.

8. Shehadeh, *The Third Way*, pp. 23–24.

9. Ibid., p. 51.

10. Khalifah, *'Abbad al-shams*, pp. 70–92.

11. Sahar Khalifah, *Wild Thorns*.

12. "Watan," in al-Qasim, *Dammi 'ala kaffi*, pp. 62–64.

13. Darwish, *Yawmiyat*, p. 40.

14. Shehadeh, *The Third Way*, p. 21.

15. "Yawmiyat jurh filastini," in Mahmud Darwish, *Diwan Mahmud Darwish*, vol. 1, p. 560.

16. Moshe Shamir, *My Life with Ishmael*, pp. 153–154.

17. Gila Ramras-Rauch, *The Arab in Israeli Literature*, pp. 86–88.

18. Shamir, *My Life with Ishmael*, p. 155.

19. Ibid., p. 158.

20. Ibid., p. 168.

21. Ibid., pp. 153–191.

22. A. B. Yehoshua, "Facing the Forests," in *Three Days and a Child*.

23. Meron Benvenisti, *Conflicts and Contradictions*, pp. 27–28.

24. Yehoshua, "Facing the Forests," p. 166.

25. Ramras-Rauch, *The Arab in Israeli Literature*, pp. 138–140.

26. Darwish, *Yawmiyat*, pp. 67–68.

27. Ramras-Rauch, *The Arab in Israeli Literature*, p. 197.

28. Ibid., p. 202, quoting from the *New York Times Book Review*, April 17, 1988.

29. Darwish, *Yawmiyat*, p. 51.

30. Ibid., p. 54.

31. Ibid., pp. 55–56.

32. Ibid., p. 56.

33. Ibid., pp. 58–59.

34. See Susan Slyomovics, "Discourses on the Pre-1948 Palestinian Village: The Case of Ein Hod/Ein Houd," *Traditional Dwellings and Settlements Review* 4 (1993): 27–37, for an in-depth analysis of this village and its various cultural meanings.

35. Darwish, *Yawmiyat*, pp. 60–61.

36. Ibid., p. 69.

37. Ibid., p. 64.

BIBLIOGRAPHY

Abu-Laban, Baha, and Ibrahim Abu-Lughod, eds. *Settler Regimes in Africa and the Arab World.* AAUG Monograph Series, no. 4. Wilmette, Ill.: Medina University Press, 1974.

Abu-Lughod, Ibrahim, ed. *The Transformation of Palestine.* Evanston, Ill.: Northwestern University Press, 1971.

Alexander, Christopher, Sara Ishikawa, and Murray Silverstein. *A Pattern Language.* New York: Oxford University Press, 1977.

Appleton, Jay. *The Experience of Landscape.* London: John Wiley, 1975.

Aruri, Naseer, and Edmund Ghareeb, eds. *Enemy of the Sun.* Washington, D.C.: Drum and Spear Press, 1970.

Ashrawi, Hanan Mikhail. "The Contemporary Palestinian Poetry of Occupation." *Journal of Palestine Studies* 7 (1978): 77–101.

al-Ashtar, 'Abd al-Karim. *Dirasat fi adab al-nakbah: al-riwayah.* Beirut: Dar al-Fikr, 1975.

Beaumont, Peter, Gerald H. Blake, and J. Malcolm Wagstaff. *The Middle East: A Geographical Study.* Chichester, England: John Wiley, 1976.

Ben-Arieh, Yehoshua. *The Rediscovery of the Holy Land in the Nineteenth Century.* Jerusalem. Magnes Press, 1979.

Benvenisti, Meron. *Conflicts and Contradictions.* New York: Villard Books, 1986.

Bisisu, Mu'in. *al-'Amal al-shi'riyah al-kamilah.* Beirut: Dar al-'Awdah, 1979.

Boullata, Issa J. "The Beleaguered Unicorn: A Study of Tawfiq Sayyigh." *Journal of Arabic Literature* 4 (1973): 69–93.

Boullata, Issa J., trans. and ed. *Modern Arab Poets: 1950–1975.* Washington, D.C.: Three Continents Press, 1976.

al-Bustani, Wadi'. *Diwan al-filastiniyat.* N.p., 1946.

Buttimer, Anne, and David Seamon, eds. *The Human Experience of Space and Place.* New York: St. Martin's Press, 1980.

Canaan, Tawfiq. "Modern Palestinian Beliefs and Practices Relating to God." *Journal of the Palestine Oriental Society* 14 (1934): 59–92.

Canaan, Tawfiq. "Mohammedan Saints and Sanctuaries in Palestine." *Journal of the Palestine Oriental Society* 4 (1923): 1–84.

Canaan, Tawfiq. "The Palestinian Arab House." *Journal of the Palestine Oriental Society* 12 (1932): 223–247; and 13 (1933): 1–83.

Canaan, Tawfiq. "Plant-Lore in Palestinian Superstition." *Journal of the Palestine Oriental Society* 8 (1928): 129–168.

Darwish, Mahmud. *Diwan Mahmud Darwish.* 2 vols. Beirut: Dar al-'Awdah, 1978.

Darwish, Mahmud. *Yawmiyat al-huzn al-'adi.* 2nd ed. Beirut: Dar al-'Awdah, 1978.

Elmessiri, Abdelwahab M., comp. and trans. *The Palestinian Wedding.* Washington, D.C.: Three Continents Press, 1982.

Flapan, Simha. *Zionism and the Palestinians.* London: Croom Helm, 1979.

Golledge, Reginald G., and Gary T. Moore, eds. *Environmental Knowing: Theories, Research, and Methods.* Stroudsburg, Pa.: Dowden, Hutchinson and Ross, 1976.

Goodman, Paul, ed. *The Jewish National Home: The Second November.* London: J. M. Dent, 1943.

Gorny, Yosef. *Zionism and the Arabs 1882–1948: A Study of Ideology.* Oxford: Clarendon, 1987.

Graham-Brown, Sarah. *Palestinians and their Society: 1880–1946.* London: Quartet Books, 1980.

Habibi, Emile. *Sudasiyat al-ayyam al-sittah.* N.p.: Dar al-Hilal, n.d.

Habiby, Emile. *The Secret Life of Saeed, the Ill-Fated Pessoptimist.* Trans. Salma Khadra Jayyusi and Trevor Le Gassick. New York: Vantage Press, 1982.

Halkin, Simon. *Modern Hebrew Literature.* 2nd ed. New York: Schocken Books, 1970.

Halkin, Simon, ed. *Zion in Jewish Literature.* New York: Herzl Press, 1961.

Heidegger, Martin. *Poetry, Language and Thought.* Trans. Albert Hofstadter. New York: Harper and Row, 1971.

Jabra, Jabra Ibrahim. *al-Bahth 'an Walid Mas'ud.* Beirut: Dar al-Adab, 1978.

Jabra, Jabra Ibrahim. "The Rebels, the Committed and the Others: Transitions in Arabic Poetry Today." *Middle East Forum* 43 (1967): 19–32.

Jayyusi, Salma Khadra. *Trends and Movements in Modern Arabic Poetry.* 2 vols. Leiden: Brill, 1977.

Jayyusi, Salma Khadra, ed. *Modern Arabian Short Stories*. New York: Columbia University Press, forthcoming.

Kanafani, Ghassan. *al-Athar al-kamilah*. 4 vols. 2nd ed. Beirut: Dar al-Tali'ah, 1980.

Kanafani, Ghassan. *Men in the Sun and other Palestinian Stories*. Trans. Hilary Kilpatrick. London: Heinemann, 1978.

al-Kayyali, 'Abd al-Rahman. *al-Shi'r al-Filastini fi nakbat filastin*. Beirut: al-Manshurat al-'Arabiyah, 1975.

Khalifah, Sahar. '*Abbad al-shams*. Beirut: Palestine Liberation Organization, 1980.

Khalifeh, Sahar. *Wild Thorns*. Trans. Trevor LeGassick and Elizabeth Fernea. London: al-Saqi, 1985.

Khouri, Mounah, and Hamid Algar, eds. *An Anthology of Modern Arabic Poetry*. Berkeley: University of California Press, 1974.

Kilpatrick, Hilary. "Tradition and Innovation in the Fiction of Ghassan Kanafani." *Journal of Arabic Literature* 7 (1976): 53–64.

Landau, Jacob M. *Abdul-Hamid's Palestine*. London: André Deutsch, 1979.

Laquer, Walter. *A History of Zionism*. New York: Schocken Books, 1976.

Lees, G. Robinson. *Village Life in Palestine*. London: Longmans, Green, 1907.

Ley, David, and Marwyn Samuels, eds. *Humanistic Geography: Problems and Prospects*. Chicago: Maaroufah Press, 1978.

Lowenthal, David. "Past Time, Present Place: Landscape and Memory." *Geographical Review* 65 (1975): 1–36.

Lowenthal, David, and Martyn Bowden, eds. *Geographies of the Mind*. New York: Oxford University Press, 1976.

Lynch, Kevin. *The Image of the City*. Cambridge, Mass.: MIT Press, 1960.

Margalit, Hannah. "Some Aspects of the Cultural Landscape of Palestine in the First Half of the Nineteenth Century." *Israel Exploration Journal* 13 (1963): 208–223.

Meinig, Donald W., ed. *The Interpretation of Ordinary Landscapes*. New York: Oxford University Press, 1980.

Migdal, Joel S. *Palestine Society and Politics*. Princeton, N.J.: Princeton University Press, 1980.

al-Naqqash, Raja'. *Mahmud Darwish: Sha'ir al-ard al-muhtallah*. N.p.: Dar al-Hilal, n.d.

Natanson, Maurice. *Literature, Philosophy and the Social Sciences*. The Hague: Martinus Nijhoft, 1962.

Norberg-Schulz, Christian. *Genius Loci: Towards a Phenomenology of Architecture*. New York: Rizzoli, 1980.

Owen, Roger, ed. *Studies in the Economic and Social History of Palestine in the Nineteenth and Twentieth Centuries.* Carbondale, Ill.: Southern Illinois University Press, 1982.

Parvin, Manoucher, and Maurie Sommer. "Dar al-Islam: The Evolution of Muslim Territoriality and its Implications for Conflict Resolution in the Middle East." *International Journal of Middle East Studies* 11 (1980): 1–21.

Peled, M. "Annals of Doom: Palestinian Literature 1917–1948." *Arabica: Revue d'études arabes* 29 (1982): 143–183.

Pocock, Douglas C. D., ed. *Humanistic Geography and Literature.* London: Croom Helm, 1981.

Polanyi, Michael. *Meaning.* Chicago: University of Chicago Press, 1975.

al-Qasim, Samih. *Dammi 'ala kaffi.* Nazareth: Matba'at wa Ufsat al-Hakim, 1967.

al-Qasim, Samih. *Dukhkhan al-barakin.* Nazareth: Matba'at wa Ufsat al-Hakim, n.d.

Ramras-Rauch, Gila. *The Arab in Israeli Literature.* Bloomington: Indiana University Press, 1989.

Rashid, Harun Hashim. *Diwan Harun Hashim Rashid.* Beirut: Dar al-'Awdah, 1981.

Relph, Edward. *Place and Placelessness.* London: Pion Press, 1976.

Rowntree, Lester, and Margaret Conkey. "Symbolism and Landscape." *Annals of the Association of American Geographers* 70 (1980): 459–474.

Salter, Christopher, and William Lloyd. *Landscape in Literature.* Resource Papers in College Geography, no. 76–3. Washington, D.C.: Association of American Geographers, 1977.

Seamon, David. *A Geography of the Lifeworld.* New York: St. Martin's Press, 1979.

Seamon, David. "The Phenomenological Contribution to Environmental Psychology." *Journal of Environmental Psychology* 2 (1982): 119–140.

Shamir, Moshe. *My Life with Ishmael.* London: Vallentine, Mitchell, 1970.

Shammas, Anton. *Arabesques.* Trans. from the Hebrew by Vivian Eden. New York: Harper and Row, 1988.

Shehadeh, Raja. *The Third Way: A Journal of Life in the West Bank.* London: Quartet Books, 1982.

Siddiq, Muhammad. *Man Is a Cause: Political Consciousness and the Fiction of Ghassan Kanafani.* Near Eastern Studies, no. 2. Seattle: University of Washington Press, 1984.

Slyomovics, Susan. "Discourses on the Pre-1948 Palestinian Village: The Case of Ein Hod/Ein Houd." *Traditional Dwellings and Settlements Review* 4 (1993): 27–37.

Slyomovics, Susan. " 'To Put One's Finger in the Bleeding Wound':

Palestinian Theatre under Israeli Censorship." *The Drama Review* 35 (1991): 18–38.

Thomson, William M. *The Land and the Book*. Grand Rapids, Mich.: Baker Book House, 1954.

Tibawi, Abdul Latif. "Visions of the Return: The Palestinian Arab Refugee in Arabic Poetry and Art." *Middle East Journal* 17 (1963): 507–526.

Tuan, Yi-Fu. "Rootedness versus Sense of Place." *Landscape* 25 (1980): 3–8.

Tuan, Yi-Fu. *Space and Place*. Minneapolis: University of Minnesota Press, 1977.

Tuan, Yi-Fu. *Topophilia: A Study of Environmental Perception, Attitudes, and Values*. Englewood Cliffs, N.J.: Prentice-Hall, 1974.

Tuqan, Fadwa. *Diwan Fadwa Tuqan*. Beirut: Dar al-'Awdah, 1978.

Tuqan, Ibrahim. *Diwan Ibrahim*. Beirut: Dar al-Adab, 1966.

Turki, Fawaz. *The Disinherited: Journal of a Palestinian Exile*. New York: Monthly Review Press, 1972.

Turki, Fawaz. "Meaning in Palestinian History: Text and Context." *Arab Studies Quarterly* 3 (1981): 371–383.

Turner, James. *The Politics of Landscape*. Oxford: Basil Blackwell, 1979.

Waterman, S. "Ideology and Events in Israeli Human Landscapes." *Geography* 64 (1979): 171–181.

Yaghi, 'Abd al-Rahman. *Hayat al-Adab al-Filastini al-Hadith*. Beirut: The Trading Office, 1968.

Yahya, Adil. "The Role of the Refugee Camps," in *Intifada*. Ed. Jamal R. Nassar and Roger Heacock. New York: Praeger, 1990, pp. 91–106.

Yehoshua, A. B. "Facing the Forests," in *Three Days and a Child*. New York: Doubleday, 1977.

Zayyad, Tawfiq. *Ashaddu 'ala aydaykum*. N.p.: Matba'at al-Ittihad, n.d.

Zayyad, Tawfiq. *Umm Durman*. Beirut: Dar al-'Awdah, n.d.

INDEX

al-'Abushi, Burhan al-Din, 37–38
Acre, 22, 54, 71
Alexander, Christopher, 4
'Allush, Layla, 6, 84, 88
Appleton, Jay, 4
'Aql, 'Abd al-Latif, 53, 83
Al-Aqsa Mosque, 38, 39
Ashrawi, Hanan, 78, 79
al-Ashtar, 'Abd al-Karim, 45
Avneri, Uri, 5

Bavli, Hillel, 15
al-Baytjalli, Iskandir Khuri, 40
Bedouins: in Hebrew literature,
    19; in Palestinian folklore, 24;
    in Palestinian literature, 58–59
Beirut, 50, 54, 60, 65
Ben Amittai, Levi, 30
Ben-Arieh, Yehoshua, 11–12
Benvenisti, Meron, 11, 31–32
Berdichevsky, Micah Joseph, 29
Bethlehem, 22, 80
Bialik, Hayyim Nahman, 29
biblical images, 10–13, 15, 19
Brenner, Yosef Haim, 20
British Mandate, 9, 13, 38
Buber, Martin, 29

al-Buraq, 38, 39
al-Bustani, Wadi', 39
Buttimer, Anne, 4

censorship, 78

Damascus, 54, 60
Darwish, Mahmud, 1–3, 62, 66,
    71–72, 77–80, 82, 83, 86, 88, 89,
    91–92, 94–98
Dayr Yasin, 76
Dome of the Rock, 38, 39
Dovey, Kim, 5

Ein Hod ('Ayn Hawd), 97
Epstein, Itzhak, 18

Fahmi, Ahmad, 45
Fanon, Franz, 79

Galilee, 11, 16, 39, 45, 49, 73, 82
Gaza, 22, 44; Gaza Strip, 49, 50,
    57, 67
geography: humanistic, 3; in
    Zionist educational curricula,
    31–32
al-ghurbah, 48, 51, 68

Ha'am, Ahad, 18
Habibi, Emile, 71, 73, 76–77
Haifa, 6, 65, 73, 82, 84, 88–89
Halkin, Simon, 30, 31
Hebrew literature, Arabs in, 19–20, 32–33, 93–94
Hebron, 22
Hehalutz (The Pioneer), 29–30; literary influence on Zionism, 30–32
Heidegger, Martin, 5
Herzl, Theodor, 16
Hittin, 39
Holocaust, 97
Holy Land, 8, 9–15, 17
Holy Sepulchre, Church of, 38–39
Husayn, Rashid, 62–63, 64, 82–83
al-Husayni, Musa, 40
al-Hut, Mahmud, 45–46, 47

Intifada, 2, 67, 78–79
Iraq, 38–39, 55–56, 60, 68
Irgun, 76

Jabra, Jabra Ibrahim, 40, 41–44, 51–52, 61–62, 80–81
Jaffa, 10, 20, 21, 45–46, 57, 63, 65, 71, 82, 92
Jerusalem, 6, 10, 20, 21, 38, 39, 45, 90
Jewish immigration to Palestine, 16–17, 19, 29
Jewish National Fund, 18
Jordan, 48, 49, 50
Josephus, 11, 12

Kafr Qasim, 76
Kanafani, Ghassan, 54–59, 65–66, 69, 88–89
Khalifah, Sahar, 91
Kuwait, 54, 55, 56

Laquer, Walter, 20–21
Lebanon, 49, 50, 68, 96

Lebenson, Micah Joseph, 15
Lees, G. Robinson, 12–13
Lynch, Kevin, 4

Mahmud, 'Abd al-Rahim, 38
Malul, Nissim, 20
mapping, 11, 33, 95
Meir, Golda, 21
Mount Carmel, 9, 71
Mount of Olives, 39

Nablus, 22, 91
al-Naqqash, Raja', 74–75
Nasir, Kamal, 46
al-Na'uri, 'Isa, 44
Nazareth, 22, 35
Nazism, 88, 97
Negev Desert, 54, 57
1948 War, 42–44, 55, 75, 88, 96

olive trees, 23, 43, 51, 56, 74–76, 78, 87, 91, 92
Ottoman Empire, 8, 9, 16; land tenure policy in Palestine, 22–23

Palestine: clothing and embroidery, 22, 43, 65; folklore, 22, 23–26; 19th century, 8–17, 22–23; travel and tourism, 9–14, 24, 91–92; Western images of, 8–15, 26; Zionist images of, 15, 16, 18, 20, 21, 26
Palestinian literature: desert imagery, 51–59, 67–68; domestic imagery, 73–77, 84; in Israel, 70–85; initial responses to Zionism, 36–42, 68; Israelis in, 44–45, 57–58, 66–67, 69, 81, 86–92, 95; nature and environmental imagery, 34–35, 40–41, 43–45, 74–76, 78–84; refugee camp imagery, 63–67,

69; relationship to classical Arabic poetry, 34; responses to exile, 42–47, 48, 51–69; rural imagery, 72–74, 77–78; sexual imagery, 83–84; urban imagery, 60–63, 68–69, 89–92

Palestinian nationalism: in literature, 36–39, 42–43; symbols, 23, 36, 39, 71–72, 74, 78–79, 83–85, 87–88

Palestinian refugees, 42, 44, 46, 48–50, 54–55, 57, 60, 63–67, 76, 96–97

PFLP (Popular Front for the Liberation of Palestine), 54

place names, 11, 89

al-Qasim, Samih, 77, 91
Qaʿwar, Najwa, 40

rain, 64–66, 80–83, 98
Rakah (Israeli Communist Party), 72
Ramras-Rauch, Gila, 19
Rashid, Harun Hashim, 44, 45
Relph, Edward, 4, 59, 68

Safed, 22, 45
Sayyigh, Tawfiq, 60
Schlonsky, Abraham, 31
Shamir, Moshe, 32–33, 92–93
Shammas, Anton, 73–75, 81, 94

Shehadeh, Raja, 2, 46, 86–88, 91–92
Shimonovitz, David, 30
Slyomovics, Susan, 78–79
Steinberg, Jacob, 30
Syria, 49, 50

Tel Aviv, 40–41, 46, 91, 93
Thomson, W. M., 11, 12, 13, 15
Tuan, Yi-Fu, 4–5, 84
Tubi, Asma, 41
Tuqan, Fadwa, 44, 53
Tuqan, Ibrahim, 37
Turki, Fawaz, 64–65, 68–69, 70
Turner, James, 14, 79

UNRWA (United Nations Relief and Works Agency), 50, 54, 64, 65

West Bank, 44, 46, 48–51, 67, 90

Yehoshua, A. B., 93–95

Zayyad, Tawfiq, 74, 75
Zionism, 15, 16–21, 28, 34, 35, 84, 94; Arab labor policy, 16, 18; education curriculum, 31–32; images of Palestine, 15–16, 18, 20–21, 29–31; Jewish labor policy, 18, 37; socialism, 17–18, 29; Zionist Congresses, 16, 18